NATIONAL ANTHEMS OF THE WORLD

NATIONAL ANTHEMS
of the
WORLD

Sixth Edition

Edited by

W.L. REED and M.J. BRISTOW

BLANDFORD PRESS
POOLE   NEW YORK   SYDNEY

First published in the U.K. 1960 by Blandford Press,
Link House, West Street, Poole, Dorset, BH15 1LL
Second edition 1963
Third edition 1969
Fourth edition 1975
Fifth edition 1978
Sixth edition 1985
Reprinted 1986

Distributed in the United States by
Sterling Publishing Co., Inc.,
2 Park Avenue, New York, N.Y. 10016

Distributed in Australia by
Capricorn Link (Australia) Pty Ltd,
PO Box 665, Lane Cove, NSW 2066

ISBN 0 7137 1525 1

Typeset by Halstan, Amersham, Buckinghamshire

Printed in Great Britain by
Butler and Tanner, Frome and London

CONTENTS

Preface

Since the Fifth Edition (1978) of this book, a number of countries have achieved independence and produced new national anthems, while others have revised their anthems. We are able to incorporate new anthems for Angola, Antigua and Barbuda, Cape Verde Islands, Comoro Islands, Djibouti, Dominica, Kiribati, Saint Kitts and Nevis, Saint Vincent and The Grenadines, São Tomé and Príncipe, Seychelles, Solomon Islands, Tuvalu and Vanuatu. The following nations have replaced their anthems — Congo, Egypt, Iran, Iraq, Kampuchea, Kuwait, Nigeria, Romania, Somalia, Thailand, Togo and Zimbabwe. We have made amendments where words and texts have changed, as in the cases of Cameroon, China, Laos, Maldives and Swaziland, whilst full texts have been acquired for New Zealand and Switzerland.

Texts have also been obtained for Ethiopia, Mongolia, Morocco, Nauru, Oman and the Yemen Arab Republic, and these have been added to the music in this edition. In a few cases, it has not been possible to place the words under the vocal lines, as no indication of this has been given in the material provided, and efforts to obtain vocal scores or recordings have not succeeded. In such cases the words have been printed separately. It is hoped that further information will be available in due course, and that performable vocal versions can be made and included in a further edition. There are, however, four anthems for which we have been unable to obtain the words — Afghanistan, Equatorial Guinea, Guinea and the Libyan Arab Jamahiriya.

Countries which are the dependent territories of other countries principally use the national anthem of the 'mother country'. It has been decided to delete anthems of dependent countries in the present edition. Exception, however, has been made in the case of the Isle of Man and Wales, which form part of the United Kingdom. The former royalist anthems of Bulgaria and Romania have also been omitted. In the case of Zimbabwe, a provisional anthem is included until a new one has been chosen.

Certain national anthems have numerous verses, only one or two of which are customarily used, and so only these are given. Where English translations have been versified to fit the music, this has been done not so much for the purpose of singing (for the original language or languages would be used), but more to offer an indication of the meaning and so help in intelligent interpretation in singing the original words.

Where an anthem is in a language that is not written in the Latin alphabet, the words are given in a transliterated phonetic version to enable the anthem to be sung by those who cannot read it in its original form.

The editors would like to express their thanks for the valuable help and advice given to them by Dr. T.M. Cartledge, a former editor of this book, who is now resident in the U.S.A.; to the members of the staff of the School of Oriental and African Studies and the BBC External Service in London, who have been responsible for the transliteration and translation of several of the African and Asian anthems; and to the Embassies and High Commissions and their staffs who have supplied much information concerning their anthems.

Acknowledgement is made at the foot of those anthem arrangements and translations which are the copyright of J.B. Cramer & Co. Ltd, and other copyright material has been similarly acknowledged. Every effort has been made to trace copyright ownership, and it is regretted if any acknowledgements have been unwittingly omitted. In most cases the version of the melody and the accompaniment is that officially authorized by the State. Where piano arrangements and translations have been specially made, these may not be reproduced without the permission of Blandford Press.

It is hoped that this Sixth Edition will be a useful source book, not only for the increasing number of occasions on which it is desired to sing or play a particular anthem, but also as a reference book of considerable interest (as the previous five editions have proved to be) and as a record of the aspirations of the whole family of nations.

W.L.R.

M.J.B.   November 1984

AFGHANISTAN

Words by SULEIMAN LAEQ (*b.* 1930)

Melody by JALĪL GHAHLĀND (*b.* 1931)
Band score arranged by
USTAD SALIM SARMAD (*b.* 1928)
Arranged for piano by W.L. REED

Adopted in 1978

10

Translation

Oh sun, become warmer and warmer,
Oh sun of Freedom and Prosperity!
Through storms we have paved the path of freedom,
The path of darkness and of light,
Reddened by military sacrifice,
Cleansed by brotherhood.
This Revolutionary country belongs to the workers.
This land, our inheritance, belongs to the farmers.
The time of oppression has passed, it is the workers' turn.
We want Peace and Brotherhood for the world.
We want complete freedom for the workers.
We want food for them, clothes and shelter.

Original words not yet available.

ALBANIA

Words by
ALEKSANDËR STAVRE DRENOVA
(1872-1947)

Music by
CIPRIAN PORUMBESCU (1853-1883)
Arr. by HENRY COLEMAN

Rreth flam - ur - it të për ba - shku - ar Me - një dë -
- shir e një që - llim; Të gjith at - je duk 'ju be -
- tu - ar Të lid - him be - sën për shpë - tim. Prej

Adopted as National Anthem, 1912
Ciprian Porumbescu also wrote the words and music of the Romanian Anthem.

Free Translation

The flag which in battle unites us
Found us all ready for the oath,
One mind, one aim, until our land
Becomes free from the enemy.
We stand in the battle for right and freedom,
The enemies of the people stand alone,
The hero dedicates his life to our land,
Even in dying he will be brave.

ALGERIA
Qassaman

Words by
MUFDI ZAKARIAH (1930-1978)

Music by
MOHAMED FAWZI (1918-1966)
Arr. by TAREK HASSAN

1. Qa - ssa - man Bin - na - zi - la - t Il - ma - hi - qat _____ Wad - di -

- maa Iz - za - ki - ya - t It - ta - hi - rat. _____ Qa - ssa -

Adopted as National Anthem in 1963.

2. *Nah-no Gon-don Fi Sa-bi-l Il hakki Thor-na*
   Wa I-la Iss-tiq-la-li-na Bil-har-bi Kum-na.
   Lam Ya-kon Yoss-gha La-na Lam-ma Na-tak-na
   Fat-ta-khath-na Ran-na-t Al-ba-roo-di Waz-na.
   Wa Azaf-na Na-gha-ma-t Al-rash-sha-shi Lah-na
   Wa A-qad-na Al-azma An Tah-ya Al-ga-za-ir.
       Fash-ha-doo! Fash-ha-doo! Fash-ha-doo!

3. *Nah-no min Ab-ta-li-na Nad-fa-oo Gon-dan*
   Wa A-la Ash-la-ina Nass-na-oo Mag-dan.
   Wa A-la Ar-wa-he-na Nass-a-do Khul-dan
   Wa A-la Ha-ma-ti-na Nar-fa-o Ban-dan.
   Gab-ha-to 'L-tah-ree-ri Aa-tay-na-ki Ah-dan
   Wa A-qad-na Al-azma An Tah-ya Al-ga-za-ir.
       Fash-ha-doo! Fash-ha-doo! Fash-ha-doo!

4. *Sar-kha-to 'l-aw-ta-ni min Sa-h Il-fi-da*
   Iss-ma-oo-ha Wass-ta-gee-bo Lin-ni-da
   Wak-to-boo-ha Bi-di-maa Il-sho-ha-daa
   Wak-ra-oo-ha Li-ba-ny Il-geeli gha-dan.
   Kad Ma-dad-na La-ka Ya Mag-do Ya-da
   Wa A-qad-na Al-azma An Tah-ya Al-ga-za-ir.
       Fash-ha-doo! Fash-ha-doo! Fash-ha-doo!

French Translation

1. *Par les foudres qui anéantissent,*
   Par les flots de sang pur et sans tache,
   Par les drapeaux flottants qui flottent,
   Sur les hauts djebels orgueilleux et fiers,
   Nous jurons nous être révoltés pour vivre ou pour mourir,
   Et nous avons juré de mourir pour que vive l'Algérie!
       Témoignez! Témoignez! Témoignez!

2. *Nous sommes des soldats pour la justice, révoltés,*
   Et pour notre indépendance nous avons engagé le combat,
   Nous n'avons obéi à nulle injonction en nous soulevant.
   Le bruit de la poudre a été notre mesure
   Et le crépitement des mitrailleuses notre chant favori.
   Et nous avons juré de mourir pour que vive l'Algérie!
       Témoignez! Témoignez! Témoignez!

3. *Sur nos héros nous bâtirons une gloire*
   Et sur nos corps nous monterons à l'immortalité,
   Sur nos âmes, nous construirons une armée
   Et de notre espoir nous lèverons l'étendard.
   Front de la libération, nous t'avons prêté serment
   Et nous avons juré de mourir pour que vive l'Algérie!
       Témoignez! Témoignez! Témoignez!

4. *Le cri de la patrie monte des champs de bataille.*
   Ecoutez-le et répondez à l'appel.
   Ecrivez-le dans le sang des martyrs
   Et dictez-le aux générations futures.
   Nous t'avons donné la main, ô gloire,
   Et nous avons juré de mourir pour que vive l'Algérie!
       Témoignez! Témoignez! Témoignez!

Translation by T. M. Cartledge
(from the French)

1. We swear by the lightning that destroys,
   By the streams of generous blood being shed,
   By the bright flags that wave,
   Flying proudly on the high djebels,
   That we are in revolt, whether to live or to die,
       We are determined that Algeria should live,
       So be our witness- be our witness- be our witness.

2. We are soldiers in revolt for truth
   And through war we try to get our Independence.
   When we spoke, nobody listened to us,
   So we have taken the noise of gunpowder as our rhythm
   And the sound of machine-guns as our melody,
       We are determined that Algeria should live,
       So be our witness- be our witness- be our witness.

3. From our heroes we shall make an army come to being,
   From our dead we shall build up a glory,
   Our spirits shall ascend to immortality
   And on our shoulders we shall raise the Standard.
   To the nation's Liberation Front we have sworn an oath,
       We are determined that Algeria should live,
       So be our witness- be our witness- be our witness.

4. The cry of the Fatherland sounds from the battle-fields.
   Listen to it and answer the call!
   Let it be written with the blood of martyrs
   And be read to future generations.
   Oh, Glory, we have held out our hand to you,
       We are determined that Algeria should live,
       So be our witness- be our witness- be our witness.

ANDORRA

Words by
JOAN BENLLOCH I VIVÓ
(1864-1926)

Music by
ENRIC MARFANY BONS
(1871-1942)

This became officially the National Anthem on the 8 September, 1914,
the anniversary day of the Jungfrau von Meritxell, patron saint of Andorra.

-ce - sa nasquí i Pu - bi - lla en - tre dos na - cions neu-

-tral;___ Sols res - to l'ú - ni - ca fi - lla del im-

-pe - ri Car - le - many. Cre - ient i lliu - re on - se

se - gles, cre - ient i lliu - re vull ser.

¡Si - guen els furs mos tu - tors i mos Prín-ceps de - fen - sors! i mos

Prín - ceps de - fen - sors!

Free Translation

The great Charlemagne, my Father, from the Saracens liberated me, and from heaven he gave me life of Meritxell the great Mother. I was born a Princess, a Maiden neutral between two nations; I am the only remaining daughter of the Carolingian empire. Believing and free eleven centuries, believing and free I will be. The laws of the land be my tutors and my defender Princes! and my defender Princes!

ANGOLA

Words by
MANUEL RUI ALVES MONTEIRO (*b.*1941)

Music by
RUI ALBERTO VIEIRA DIAS MINGAS (*b.*1939)
Harmonised and arranged by W.L. REED

Martially

1. O Pá - tria, nun - ca mais es - que - ce - re - mos os he-

ró is do qua - tro de Fe - ve - rei - o. O

Pá - tria, nós sau - da - mos os teus fi - lhos tom -

Adopted in 1975.

in - do no Tra - bal - ho o Ho - mem no - vo. An - go - la, a-

van - te! Re - vo - lu - ção, pe - lo Po - der Po - pu-

lar! Pá - tria U - ni - da, Li - ber - da - de, um só

Po - vo, u - ma só Na - ção! An - go - la, a - van - te! Re - vo - lu-

ção,   pe - lo Po - der Po - pu - lar!   Pá - tria U -

ni - da, Li - ber - da - de, um só Po - vo, u -ma só Na - ção!

Translation

2. *Levantemos nossas vozes libertadas*
    para glória dos povos africanos.
    Marchemos, combatentes angolanos,
    solidários com os povos oprimidos.
    Orgulhosos lutaremos pela Paz
    com as forças progressistas do mundo.
    Orgulhosos lutaremos pela Paz
    com as forças progressistas do mundo

    Angola, avante!
    Revolução, pelo Poder Popular!
    Pátria Unida, Liberdade,
    um só Povo, uma só Nação!

1. O Fatherland, we shall never forget
    the heroes of the Fourth of February.
    O Fatherland, we salute your sons
    who died for our Independence.
    We honour the past and our history
    as by our work we build the New Man.

    Forward, Angola!
    Revolution through the power of the People!
    A United Country, Freedom,
    One People, one Nation!

2. Let us raise our liberated voices
    to the glory of the peoples of Africa.
    We shall march, Angolan fighters,
    in solidarity with oppressed peoples.
    We shall fight proudly for Peace
    along with the progressive forces of the world.

    Forward, Angola! etc.

ANTIGUA and BARBUDA

Words by
NOVELLE HAMILTON RICHARDS (*b*.1917)

Music by
WALTER GARNET PICART CHAMBERS (*b*.1908)

Not too fast

mf

1. Fair An - ti - gua, we sa - lute thee! Proud - ly we this an - them raise
2. Raise the stan - dard! Raise it bold - ly! Ans - wer now to du - ty's call
3. God of na - tions, let Thy bless - ings Fall up - on this land of ours;

To thy glo - ry____ and thy beau - ty, Joy - ful - ly we sing the praise
To the ser - vice____ of thy coun - try, Spar - ing noth - ing, giv - ing all;
Rain and sun - shine____ ev - er send - ing, Fill her fields with crops and flowers;

Of the vir - tues, all be - stow - èd On thy sons and daugh - ters free;
Gird your loins and join the bat - tle 'Gainst fear, hate and pov - er - ty,
We her chil - dren do im - plore Thee, Give us strength, faith, loy - al - ty,

Ev - er striv - ing, ev - er seek - ing,____ Dwell in love and un - i - ty.
Each en - dea - vour - ing, all a - chiev - ing,____ Live in peace where man is free.
Nev - er fail - ing, all en - dur - ing____ To de - fend her lib - er - ty.

Originally adopted in 1967 on achieving statehood, and again in 1981 when achieving independence.

ARGENTINA

Words by
VICENTE LÓPEZ Y PLANES
(1785-1856)

Music by
BLAS PARERA (1765- c. 1830)
Arr. by **JUAN PEDRO ESNAOLA (1808-1878)**

Officially adopted as National Anthem, 11 May, 1813, by the General Constituent Assembly.

li - bres del mun - do res - pon - den: ¡Al gran

pue - blo Ar-gen-ti - no, Sa - lud!____ ¡Al gran

pue - blo Ar-gen-ti - no, Sa - lud! Y____ los

li - bres del mun - do res - pon - den ¡Al gran

pue - blo Ar-gen - ti - no, Sa - lud!　　Y___ los

li - bres del mun - do res - pon - den　　¡Al gran

pue - blo Ar-gen - ti - no, Sa - lud!

CHORUS
Allegro vivace

Sean e-ter-nos los lau-re-les. Que su-pi-mos con-se-

-guir: Que su-pi-mos con-se-guir: Co-ro-

-na-dos de glo-ria vi-va---mos O__ ju-

-re-mos con glo-ria mo-rir. O ju-

Free Translation

Hear, oh mortals! the sacred cry:
Freedom, freedom, freedom!
Hear the noise of broken chains;
See the throne of Equality the noble.

The United Provinces of the South
Their throne full of dignity opened!
And the free of the world reply:
A salutation to the great Argentine people!

CHORUS Let those laurels be eternal
Which we knew how to win:
Let us live crowned by glory
Or swear with glory to die.

AUSTRALIA

Words and music by
PETER DODDS McCORMICK (1834-1916)

Maestoso

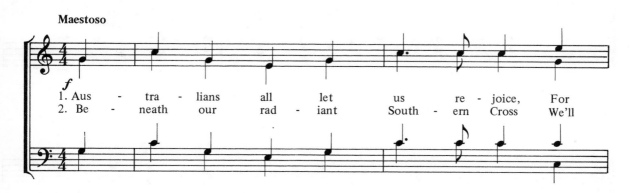

1. Aus - tra - lians all let us re - joice, For
2. Be - neath our rad - iant South - ern Cross We'll

we are young and free; We've gold - en soil and
toil with hearts and hands; To make this Com - mon -

wealth for toil, Our home is girt by sea. Our
wealth of ours Re - nowned of all the lands; For

Adopted as the National Anthem officially in 1984. The words were then slightly changed.

34

AUSTRIA

Words by
PAULA PRERADOVIĆ (1887-1951)

Music by
JOHANN HOLZER (1753-1818)*
Arr. by VIKTOR KELDORFER

1. Land der Ber - ge, Land am Stro - me, Land der Äk - ker, Land der Do - me, Land der Häm - mer, zu - kunfts - reich! Hei - mat bist du gro - sser Söh - ne,

2. Heiss um feh - det, wild um strit - ten, liegst dem Erd - teil du in - mit - ten ei - nem star - ken Her - zen gleich. Hast seit frü - hen Ah - nen - ta - gen

Officially adopted as National Anthem by Austrian Cabinet 25 February, 1947.
*Mozart has been claimed as the composer, but the evidence is more in Holzer's favour,
according to Austrian scholarship.

Volk, be - gna - det für das Schö-ne, Viel - ge - rühm - tes
ho - her Sen - dung Last ge - tra - gen, Viel - ge - prüf - tes

Ö - ster - reich. Viel - ge - rühm - tes_ Ö - ster - reich.
Ö - ster - reich. Viel - ge - prüf - tes_ Ö - ster - reich.

3. *Mutig in die neuen Zeiten,*
   frei und gläubig sieh uns schreiten,
   arbeitsfroh und hoffnungsreich.
   Einig lass in Bruderchören,
   Vaterland, dir Treue schwören,
   Vielgeliebtes Österreich. (bis)

Free Translation

1. Land of mountains, land of streams, land of fields,
   land of spires, land of hammers, with a rich future,
   you are the home of great sons, a nation blessed
   by its sense of beauty,
   highly praised Austria, highly praised Austria,

2. Strongly fought for, fiercely contested, you are
   in the centre of the Continent like a strong heart,
   you have borne since the earliest days the burden
   of a high mission,
   much tried Austria, much tried Austria.

3. Watch us striding free and believing, with courage,
   into new eras, working cheerfully and full of hope,
   in fraternal chorus let us take in unity the oath
   of allegiance to you, our country,
   our much beloved Austria, our much beloved Austria.

BAHAMAS

Words and Music by
TIMOTHY GIBSON (1903-1978)
Arr. by W.L. REED

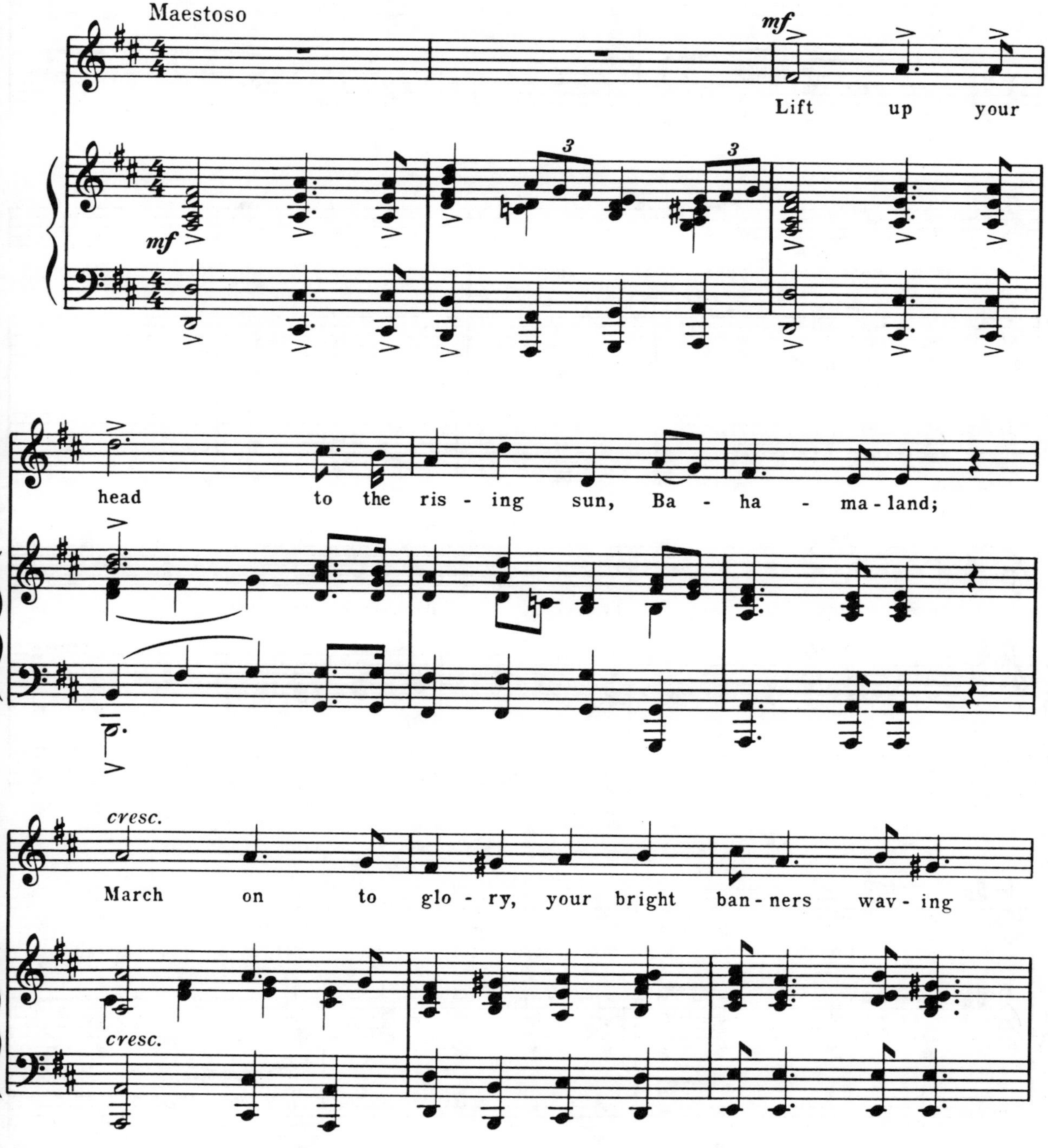

Maestoso
mf
Lift up your
mf
3
3
head to the ris - ing sun, Ba - ha - ma - land;
cresc.
March on to glo - ry, your bright ban - ners wav - ing
cresc.

Selected as a result of a competition and adopted when the country became independent on July 10, 1973.

38

BAHRAIN

No words

Composer unknown
Amended and arranged by
MOHAMMED SUDQI AYYASH (b. 1925)

This amended version was adopted in 1971.

BANGLADESH

Music supervised by
SAMAR DAS

Words and music by
RABINDRANATH TAGORE (1861-1941)*
Arr. by T.M. CARTLEDGE

Officially adopted in April 1971 by the then provisional government;
approved by the National Assembly on 13 January 1972.
* Rabindranath Tagore also wrote the words and music of the Indian National Anthem.

Translation by Professor Syed Ali Ahsan

My Bengal of gold, I love you.
Forever your skies, your air set my heart in tune
As if it were a flute.
In spring, O mother mine, the fragrance from your mango groves
Makes me wild with joy —
Ah, what a thrill!

In autumn, O mother mine,
In the full-blossomed paddy fields
I have seen spread all over — sweet smiles.
Ah, what a beauty, what shades, what an affection
And what a tenderness!
What a quilt have you spread at the feet of banyan trees
And along the banks of rivers!

O mother mine, words from your lips
Are like nectar to my ears.
Ah, what a thrill!
If sadness, O mother mine, casts a gloom on your face,
My eyes are filled with tears!

BARBADOS

Words by
IRVING LOUIS BURGIE (*b.* 1924)

Music by
VAN ROLAND EDWARDS (*b.* 1912)

1. In __ plen-ty and in time of need When this fair land was young, Our __ brave fore-fa-thers sowed the seed From which our pride is sprung, A pride that makes no wan-ton boast Of what it has with-

2. The __ Lord has been the peo-ple's guide For past three hun-dred years. With __ Him still on the peo-ple's side We have no doubts or fears. Up-ward and on-ward we shall go, In-spired, ex-ult-ing,

This anthem was adopted on 30 November, 1966, upon independence.

BELGIUM

La Brabançonne

Words by
CHARLES ROGIER (1800-1885)
English translation of the French words by
MARY ELIZABETH SHAW and DICCON SHAW

Music by
FRANÇOIS VAN CAMPENHOUT (1779-1848)

Fieramente, non allegro

A-près des siè - cles__ d'es - cla - va - ge, Le__
O dier - baar Bel - gië, o heil - ig land der vaa - dren, on - ze
From out the tomb of __ bond - age and sla - ve - ry Has__

Bel - ge, sor - tant du tom - beau, A re - con-
ziel en ons hart zijn U ge - wijd. Aan-vaard ons
Bel - gium at last ris - en free; And has re-

- quis par__ son__ cou - ra - ge Son__
kracht en het bloed__ van ons aa - dren, wees ons
- cov - ered __ by__ her __ bra - ve - ry, Her__

Written and composed during the 1830 revolution. The original French words were by Jenneval, a Belgian officer, but the present version was written in 1860 by Prime Minister Charles Rogier. The Dutch text also underwent several changes. The present version was officially adopted in 1938 — it is a different text from the French.

BELIZE

Words by
SAMUEL ALFRED HAYNES (1898-1971)

Music by
SELWYN WALFORD YOUNG (1899-1977)
Arranged from orchestral version by
W.L. REED

1. O, Land of the Free by the Carib Sea, Our manhood we pledge to thy liberty! No tyrants here linger, despots must flee This

2. Nature has blessed thee with wealth untold, O'er mountains and valleys where prairies roll; Our fathers, the Baymen, valiant and bold Drove

back the ty - rants, let des - pots _____ flee!

Land of the Free by the Ca -

allargando

allargando

rib Sea!

BENIN

L'Aube Nouvelle
(The Dawn of a New Day)

Words and music by
GILBERT DAGNON (*b.* 1926)
Arr. by HENRY COLEMAN

Adopted as the National Anthem of Dahomey at the declaration of independence, August, 1960.
The change of name to Bénin took place on 30 November, 1975.

The chorus is usually sung on its own.

-vrer au prix du sang des com - bats é - cla - tants. Ac-cou-

-rez vous aus-si, bâ - tis - seurs du pré - sent, Plus forts dans

l'u - ni - té, chaqu' jour à la tâ - che, Pour la

pos - té - ri - té, cons - trui - sez sans re - lâ - che.

CHORUS

En - fants du Bé - nin, de - bout! La li - ber - té d'un cri so - no - re Chante aux pre-miers feux de l'au- ro - re; En-fants du Bé - nin, de - bout!

2. *Quand partout souffle un vent de colère et de haine,*
   Béninois, sois fier, et d'une âme sereine,
   Confiant dans l'avenir, regarde ton drapeau!
   Dans le vert tu liras l'espoir du renouveau,
   De tes aïeux le rouge évoque le courage;
   Des plus riches trésors le jaune est le présage.

3. *Tes monts ensoleillés, tes palmiers, ta verdure,*
   Cher Bénin, partout font ta vive parure.
   Ton sol offré à chacun la richesse des fruits.
   Bénin, désormais que tes fils tous unis
   D'un fraternel élan partagent l'espérance
   De te voir à jamais heureux dans l'abondance.

Paraphrase by
Elizabeth P. Coleman

Chorus

Children of Bénin, arise!
The resounding cry of freedom
Is heard at the first light of dawn;
Children of Bénin, arise!

1. Formerly, at her call, our ancestors
   Knew how to engage in mighty battles
   With strength, courage, ardour, and full of joy, but at the price of blood.
   Builders of the present, you too, join forces
   Each day for the task stronger in unity
   Build without ceasing for posterity.

2. When all around there blows a wind of anger and hate:
   Citizen of Bénin be proud, and in a calm spirit
   Trusting in the future, behold your flag!
   In the green you read hope of spring;
   The red signifies the courage of your ancestors;
   The yellow foretells the richest treasures.

3. Beloved Bénin, your sunny mountains, palm trees, and green pastures
   Show everywhere your brightness;
   Your soil offers everyone the richest fruits.
   Bénin, from henceforth your sons are united
   With one brotherly spirit sharing the hope of seeing you
   Enjoy abundance and happiness for ever.

BHUTAN

Music by
DASHO THINLEY DORJI
Transcribed and arranged by
W.L. REED

61

BOLIVIA

Words by
JOSÉ IGNACIO de SANJINES (1821-1865)
Translation by G.H. HATCHMAN
Versified by SEBASTIAN SHAW

Music by
LEOPOLDO BENEDETTO VINCENTI
(1815-1914)

Allegro marziale

VERSE

1. *Bo - li - via - nos: el ha - do pro-*
1. Oh Bo - li - via, our long felt de-

-pi - cio co - ro - nó___ nues - tros vo - tos y an - he - lo; es ya
-sires,___ By the kind - li-ness of des - ti - ny are crowned now. Here, where

Played for first time in 1842 and adopted the same year.
By permission J.B. Cramer & Co. Ltd.

an - tes que es-cla - vos vi-vir!
death than ex-is - tence as slaves!

2. Esta tierra inocente y hermosa
    que ha debido a Bolívar su nombre,
    es la Patria feliz donde el hombre
    goza el bien de la dicha y la paz.
    Que los hijos del grande Bolívar
    han ya mil y mil veces jurado
    morir antes que ver humillado
    de la Patria el augusto pendón.

    CORO: De la Patria etc.

3. Loor eterno a los bravos guerreros
    cuyo heróico valor y firmeza
    conquistaron las glorias que empieza
    hoy Bolivia feliz a gozar.
    Que sus nombres el mármol y el bronce
    a remotas edades trasmitan
    y en sonoros cantares repitan
    ¡Libertad, Libertad, Libertad!

    CORO: De la Patria etc.

2. Here where Justice has raised up her throne,
    Long denied her by the evil of oppression,
    Her flung banners find glorious expression
    We are free, we are free, we are free!
    Sons, whom mighty Bolivar shall call his own,
    Have a thousand thousand times in great solemnity
    Freely offered life itself as sworn indemnity,
    If dishonoured their flag should ever be.

    CHORUS: Evermore, Motherland etc.

3. Those brave warriors eternally praise,
    Whose courage, unexampled, evermore is
    The foundation of all the proud glories
    To which happy Bolivia is heir.
    Lettered bronze and marble gratefully we'll raise
    That their deeds may live for distant generations,
    And our sons' and grandsons' joyful salutations
    Shall, in song, honour still the great names there.

    CHORUS: Evermore, Motherland etc.

BOTSWANA

Words and music by
KGALEMANG TUMEDISCO MOTSETE
(1900-1974)

Officially adopted 30 September, 1966, upon independence.

BOURKINA FASO

Words and music by
ROBERT OUEDRAOGO (*b.* 1922)
Arr. by HENRY COLEMAN

Moderato

1. Fiè - re Vol - ta de mes A - ïeux, Ton so - leil ar - dent et glo - ri - eux

Te re - vêt d'or et de clar - té, O, Rei - ne dra - pée de lo - yau - té.

CHORUS

Nous te fe - rons et plus forte et plus bel - le,

Formerly Upper Volta. The name of the country was changed on 4 August, 1984.
Approved as the National Anthem by the Upper Volta National Assembly on 3 August, 1960.
A new National Anthem is expected.

A ton a-mour, nous res-te-rons fi-dè-les, Et nos cœurs, vi-

-brants de fier-té, Ac-cla-me-ront ta beau-té. -té.

2. Vers l'horizon lève les yeux,
   Frémis aux accents tumultueux
   De tes fiers enfants tous dressés,
   Promesse d'avenirs caressés.

3. Le travail de ton sol brûlant
   Sans fin trempera les cœurs ardents,
   Et les vertus de tes enfants
   Le ceindront d'un diadème triomphant.

4. Que Dieu te garde en sa bonté,
   Que du bonheur de ton sol aimé,
   L'Amour des frères soit la clé,
   Honneur, Unité et Liberté.

Free Translation by Elizabeth P. Coleman

CHORUS   We will make thee stronger and more beautiful,
         We will stay faithful to thy love,
         And our hearts, beating with pride,
         Will acclaim thy beauty.

1. Proud Volta of my forefathers,
   Thy glorious burning sun
   Clothes thee in golden light,
   O Queen draped in loyalty.

2. Raise thine eyes towards the future
   Vibrating with tumultuous voices
   Of thy proud children, standing ready,
   The promise of a happy future.

3. The toil on thy burning soil
   Will never cease to brace the fervent hearts,
   And the virtues of thy children
   Will circle it with a triumphal crown.

4. May God protect thee in His goodness;
   For the happiness of thy beloved land,
   May brotherly love be the key
   And honour, unity and liberty.

BRAZIL

Words by
JOAQUIM OSÓRIO DUQUE ESTRADA (1870-1927)
Translation by GASTRO NOTHMAN
Versified by SEBASTIAN SHAW

Music by
FRANCISCO MANUEL da SILVA
(1795-1865)

The music was written for the National Anthem in 1831 on the accession of Emperor D. Pedro II.
In 1922 a new text was officially adopted and the same tune retained.
By permission of J.B. Cramer & Co. Ltd.

2. *Deitado eternamente em berço esplêndido,*
    Ao som do mar e à luz do céu profundo,
    Fulguras, Brasil, florão da América,
    Iluminado ao sol do novo mundo.
    Do que a terra mais garrida
    Teus risonhos, lindos campos têm mais flores,
    Nossos bosques têm mais vida,
    Nossa vida no teu seio mais amores.
        Oh! Pátria amada, idolatrada,
        Salve! Salve!
    Brasil, de amor eterno seja o símbolo
    O lábaro que ostentas estrelado,
    E diga o verde louro dessa flámula
    Paz no futuro e glória no passado.
    Mas, se ergues da justiça a clava forte
    Verás que um filho teu não foge à luta
    Nem teme quem te adora a própria morte.
        Terra adorada entre, outras mil, és tu, Brasil,
        Oh! Pátria amada! dos filhos deste solo és mãe gentil,
        Pátria amada, Brasil!

2. To ocean's music, under skies of deepest blue,
    America's fair flower, fading never,
    In splendour you lie cradled. Oh Brazil, on you
    The sun of this New World shines down for ever!
    Oh, far more than in fair lands elsewhere,
    Your sweet pastures are bedecked with smiling blossom;
    Your vast woodlands a greater life share,
    And a deeper love we know within your bosom.
        Oh glorious and beloved land, hail! Hail Brazil!
    Then let your starry ensign never cease to fly,
    Symbolic of the love that fills your story;
    And let the verdant laurels on your pennon cry :-
    "In future peace and in the past great glory!"
    But if, in justice, you should raise your mighty sword,
    You shall not see a son of yours from battle flee,
    Nor shall he fear to die for you, whom he adored.
        Amongst a thousand,
        You ever will
        Be, oh Brazil,
        The one dear homeland!
        Oh bounteous mother, with such love you fill
        Your proud children, Brazil!

BRUNEI

Words by
**PENGIRAN HAJI MOHAMED YUSUF bin
PENGIRAN HAJI ABDUL RAHIM** (*b.* 1923)

Music by
AWANG HAJI BESAR bin SAGAP (*b.* 1914)
Arr. by HENRY COLEMAN

Ya Al - lah lan - jut - kan lah u - si - a

Du - li tu - an - ku yang ma - ha mu - li - a

A - dil ber - dau - lat me - naung - i no - sa

This anthem was composed in 1947 through the initiative of a group of youths who decided that their country should have a National Anthem, and chose two of their number to write and compose it.
It was officially adopted in 1951. Brunei became independent on 1 January, 1984.

Me - mim - pin ra'a - yat ke - kal baha - gi - a;

Hi - dup sen - to - sa Ne - ga - ra dan Sul-tan,

I - la - hi se - la - mat - kan Bru - nei Da - rus sa-lam.

Free Translation

Oh God, Long Live our Majesty the Sultan;
Justice and Sovereignty in sheltering our
country and leading our people;
Prosperity to our Nation and Sultan.
God Save Brunei.

BULGARIA

Words and music by
TZVETAN RADOSLAVOV (1863-1931)

Andante maestoso (♩ = 66)

𝄋 VERSE

1. *Gor - da Sta - ra pla - nee - na, do ne-yee Doo - na - va see-ne-yee, slun - tse Tra-kee-ya o - grya - va nad Pe-ree - na pla - men - e-yee.*
2. *Pad - na ha bor - tsee bez-chet za na - ro - da nash lyu-bim. Ma-yee - ko, da-yee nee muzh - ka see - la put-ya eem da pro - dul - zheem!*
3. *Droozh - no, brat - ya Bul - ga-ree, s nas Mos - kva e v meer i v bo - yee! Par - tee - ya ve - lee - ka vo - dee nash - ee-ya po - bye - den stro-yee!*

Original words and music were composed by Radoslavov while still a student in 1885, and on his way to fight in the Serbo-Bulgarian War. It quickly became popular. It was arranged as the National Anthem, replacing the previous Republican Anthem in 1964. Both words and music have been revised many times since 1885.

Translation by Katya Boyadjieva

1. Proudly rise the Balkan peaks,
   At their feet Blue Danube flows;
   Over Thrace the sun is shining,
   Pirin looms in purple glow.

   CHORUS
   Oh, dear native land,
   Earthly paradise!
   For your loveliness, your beauty
   E'er will charm our eyes.

2. Countless warriors bravely fell
   For the people's sacred cause;
   Give us strength and firmness, Mother,
   Guide us on the road they chose.
                              CHORUS

3. Be as one, Bulgarians!
   Moscow stands by us again;
   For our valiant Party leads us
   On to victory and fame!
                              CHORUS

BURMA

English versification by
T.M. CARTLEDGE

Words and music by
SAYA TIN (1914-1947)
Arr. by W.L. REED

This officially became the National Anthem in 1948

* The notes between asterisks may be sung an octave higher.

★ At the end of the anthem it is customary for the singers to give a slight bow.

BURUNDI

Words by a commission presided over by
JEAN-BAPTISTE NTAHOKAJA (*b.* 1920)

Music prepared by
MARC BARENGAYABO
Arr. by W.L. REED

Burundi bwacu, Burundi buhire
Shinga icumu mu mashinga
Gaba intahe y'ubugabo ku bugingo
Warapfunywe ntiwapfuye,
Warahabishijwe ntiwahababuka
Uhagurukana, uhagurukana, uhagurukana ubugabo urikukira
Komerwa amashyi n'amakungu
Habwa impundu n'abawe
Isamirane mu mashinga, isamirane mu mashinga,
Burundi bwacu, ragi ry'abasokuru
Ramutswa intahe n'ibuhugu
Ufatanije ishyaka n'ubuhizi
Vuza impundu wiganzuye uwakuganza
Burundi bwacu, nkora-mutima kuri twese
Tugutuye amoboko, umutima n'ubuzima
Imana yakuduhaye ikudutungire
Horana ubumwe n'abagabo n'itekane
Sagwa n'urweze, sagwa n'amahoro meza.

French Translation by Jean-Baptiste Ntahokaja

Cher Burundi, ô doux pays,
Prends place dans le concert des nations.
En tout bien, tout honneur, accéde á l'indépendance.
Mutilé et meurtri, tu es demeuré maître de toi-même.
L'heure venue, tu t'es levé
Et fièrement tu t'es hissè au rang des peuples libres.
Reçois donc le compliment des nations,
Agrée l'hommage de tes enfants.
Qu'à travers l'univers retentisse ton nom.
Cher Burundi, héritage sacré de nos aïeux,
Reconnu digne de te gouverner,
Au courage tu allies le sentiment de l'honneur.
Chante la gloire de ta liberté reconquise.
Cher Burundi, digne objet de notre plus tendre amour,
A ton noble service nous vouons nos bras, nos coeurs et nos vies.
Veuille Dieu, qui nous a fait don de toi, te conserver à notre vénération,
Sous l'égide de l'Unité,
Dans la paix, la joie et la prospérité.

English Translation (of French Version) by T.M. Cartledge

Beloved Burundi, gentle country,
Take your place in the concert of nations,
Acceding to independence with honourable intentions.
Wounded and bruised, you have remained master of yourself.

When the hour came, you arose,
Lifting yourself proudly into the ranks of free peoples.
Receive, then, the congratulations of the nations
And the homage of your sons.
May your name ring out through the universe.

Beloved Burundi, sacred heritage from our forefathers,
Recognised as worthy of self-government,
With your courage you also have a sense of honour.
Sing the glory of liberty conquered again.

Beloved Burundi, worthy of our tenderest love,
We vow to your noble service our hands and hearts and lives.
May God, who gave you to us, keep you for us to venerate,
Under the shield of unity.
In peace, joy and prosperity.

CAMEROON
Chant de Ralliement

Words * (see footnote)

English versification
by T. M. CARTLEDGE

Music by
SAMUEL MINKIO BAMBA
and MOÏSE NYATTE NKO'O (1910-1978)
Arr. by HENRY COLEMAN

Tempo di marcia

1. O Ca - me - roun, ber - ceau de nos an - cê - tres, Va, de -
2. Tu es la tombe où dor - ment nos pè - res, Le jar -
1. O Ca - me - roon, thou cra - dle of our fa - thers, Proud-ly
2. You are the tomb where our fath - ers are rest - ing, You're the

bout, et ja - loux de ta li - ber - té. Comme un so -
din que nos aï - eux ont cul - ti - vé. Nous tra - vail -
ral - ly to de - fend your lib - er - ty. And like the
gar - den they pre - pared and they con - ceived, We work that

---

* This anthem was written and composed in 1928 by RENÉ JAM AFAME and a group of students from L'Ecole Normale de la Mission Presbytérienne Américaine de Foulassi à Sangmelina, Cameroun. It was adopted as the unofficial National Anthem in 1948 and became the official Anthem on 10th May, 1957. The words were substantially changed in 1978.

l'Est à l'Ou - est soient tout a - mour! ___ Te ser - vir
pro - gres - se ___ *tou - jours en paix,* ___ Es - pê - rant
East and West to give their heart, ___ Their on - ly
stead - i - ly ___ in ___ peace, ___ In hope that

que ce soit ___ leur ___ seul ___ but Pour ___
que tes jeu ___ nes ___ en ___ fants T'ai -
wish ___ to serve ___ their ___ land And ___ with
ev - 'ry young ___ child ___ of ___ yours Will ___

rem - plir leur de - voir tou - jours.
me - ront sans bornes à ja - mais.
con - stan - cy play their part.
love you un - til time shall ___ cease.

CANADA

Words by
Sir ADOLPHE BASILE ROUTHIER (1839-1920)
English version by
ROBERT STANLEY WEIR (1856-1926)

Music by
CALIXA LAVALLÉE (1842-1891)
Arr. by H.A. CHAMBERS

1. *O Ca - na - da!* Ter -
2. *Sous l'œil de Dieu, près*
1. O Can - a - da! Our
2. O Can - a - da! Where

-*re de nos aï - eux,*   *Ton front est ceint de*
du fleu - ve gé - ant,   *Le Ca - na - dien gran -*
home and na - tive land!   True pa - triot love in
pines and ma - ples grow,   Great prair - ies spread and

(CHORUS, S.A.T.B. *ad lib.* in English)

Et ta va - leur, de foi trem - pé - e,
Tou - jours gui - dé par sa lu - miè - re,
God keep our land, Glo - rious and free!

God keep our land,

Pro - té - ge - ra nos foy - ers et nos droits,
Il gar - de - ra l'hon - neur de son dra - peau,
O Can - a - da! We stand on guard for thee,

Pro - té - ge - ra nos foy - ers et nos___ droits.
Il gar - de - ra l'hon - neur de son dra___ peau.
O Can - a - da! We stand on guard for___ thee.

3.   *De son patron, précurseur du vrai Dieu,*
      Il porte au front l'auréole de feu.
      Ennemi de la tyrannie Mais plein de loyauté,
      Il veut garder dans l'harmonie, Sa fière liberté;
      Et par l'effort de son génie, Sur notre sol asseoir la vérité,
      Sur notre sol asseoir la vérité.

4.   *Amour sacré du trône et de l'autel,*
      Remplis nos coeurs de ton souffle immortel!
      Parmi les races étrangères, Notre guide est la loi:
      Sachons être un peuple de frères, Sous le joug de la foi.
      Et répétons, comme nos pères, Le cri vainqueur: "Pour le Christ et le roi,"
      Le cri vainqueur: "Pour le Christ et le roi."

3. O Canada! Beneath thy shining skies
   May stalwart sons and gentle maidens rise
   To keep thee steadfast thro' the years
   From East to Western sea,
   Our own beloved native land,
   Our True North strong and free!

4. Ruler supreme, Who hearest humble pray'r,
   Hold our Dominion in Thy loving care.
   Help us to find, O God, in Thee
   A lasting rich reward,
   As waiting for the better day,
   We ever stand on guard.

CAPE VERDE ISLANDS

Words and music by
AMILCAR CABRAL (1924-1973)

Allegro moderato, alla marcia

1. Sol, su - or e o ver-de e mar, ___ Sé - cu-los de dor e es-peran-ça:
2. Ra - mos do mes-mo tron-co, Ol - hos na mes-ma luz:

Es - ta é a ter - ra dos nos-sos a- vós! Fru - to das nos-sas mãos,
Es - ta é a for - ça da nos-sa u-nião! Can - tem o mar e a ter-ra

This anthem is the same as that of Guinea-Bissau.
A new National Anthem is expected.

Da flôr do nos - so san - gue: Es - ta é a nos - sa pá - tria a -
A ma - dru - ga - da e o sol___ Que a nos - sa lu - ta fe - cun -

ma - da.
dou.___ } Vi - va a pá - tri - a glo - ri - o - sa! Flo -

riu nos céus a ban - dei - ra da lu - ta. A - van - te, con - tra o

ju - go es - tran - gei - ro! Nós va - mos cons - tru - ir Na

Translation

1. Sun, sweat, verdure and sea,
   Centuries of pain and hope;
   This is the land of our ancestors.
   Fruit of our hands,
   Of the flower of our blood:
   This is our beloved country.

2. Branches of the same trunk,
   Eyes in the same light;
   This is the force of our unity!
   The sea and the land,
   The dawn and the sun are singing
   That our struggle has borne fruit!

Chorus   Long live our glorious country!
The banner of our struggle
Has fluttered in the skies.
Forward, against the foreign yoke!
We are going to build
Peace and progress
In our immortal country!

CENTRAL AFRICAN REPUBLIC

La Renaissance

Words by
BARTHÉLÉMY BOGANDA (1910-1959)

Music by
HERBERT PEPPER (*b.* 1912)

O Cen-tra-fri-que, ô berceau des Bantous!

Re - prends ton droit au res - pect, à la vie!

Long - temps sou - mis, long - temps bri - mé par tous,

Mais de ce jour bri - sant la ty - ran - nie.

This National Anthem was adopted by the National Assembly on 25 May, 1960.
The words are by the first President of the Central African Republic.
Herbert Pepper also wrote the music of the Senegal National Anthem.

Dans le tra-vail, l'ordre et la di-gni-té,

Tu re-con-quiers ton droit, ton u-ni-té,

Et pour fran-chir cette é-ta-pe nou-vel-le,

De nos an-cê-tres la voix nous ap-pel-le.

CHORUS

Au tra-vail dans l'ordre et la di-gni-té, Dans le res-pect du

droit dans l'u-ni-té, Bri-sant la mi-sè - re et la ty-ran-nie,

Brandissant l'é-ten-dard _____ de la Pa-trie. _____

Translation by
T.M. Cartledge

Oh! Central Africa, cradle of the Bantu!
Take up again your right to respect, to life!
Long subjugated, long scorned by all,
But, from today, breaking tyranny's hold.
Through work, order and dignity
You reconquer your rights, your unity,
And to take this new step
The voice of our ancestors calls us.

Chorus

To work! In order and dignity,
In the respect for rights and in unity,
Breaking poverty and tyranny,
Holding high the flag of the Fatherland.

CHAD

Words by
LOUIS GIDROL (*b.* 1922)
and students of St. Paul's School

Music by
PAUL VILLARD (*b.* 1899)
Arr. by Col. P. DUPONT

Peu - ple Tcha-dien, de - bout et à l'ou-vra - ge! Tu as con-

- quis ta terre et ton droit; Ta li - ber - té naî-

This anthem was composed for the proclamation of independence in January, 1960.

yeux, pa - ci - fique, a - vance en chan-tant, Fi - dèle à tes an -

ciens qui te re - gar - - - - dent.

Translation by
T.M. Cartledge

CHORUS

People of Chad, arise and take up the task!
You have conquered the soil and your rights;
Your freedom will be born of your courage.
Lift up your eyes, the future is yours.

VERSE

Oh, my Country, may God protect you,
May your neighbours admire your children.
Joyful, peaceful, advance as you sing,
Faithful to your fathers who are watching you.

Repeat Chorus

CHILE

Words by
EUSEBIO LILLO (1826-1910)

Music by
RAMÓN CARNICER (1789-1855)

Music was adopted 17 September, 1847. The date of the words was 12 August, 1909 and it was recognised officially as the National Anthem on 27 June, 1941. There are 5 verses; the fifth verse is that usually sung (as given here).

CHINA
People's Republic of China

Words written collectively

Music by
NIEH ERH (1912-1935)

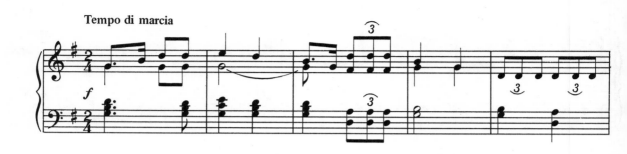

Qian jin! ge min zu ying xiong de ren min. Wei da de

gong chan dang ling dao wo men ji xu chang zheng. Wan zhong yi xin,

This song was written in 1932. On 27 September, 1949 it was officially approved as the National Anthem.
New words were adopted on 5 March, 1978.

Translation

March on, brave people of our nation!
Our Communist Party leads us on a new Long March.
Millions as one, march on, towards the communist goal!
Build our country, guard our country!
We will work and fight.
March on, March on, March on!
For ever and ever, raising Mao Tse-tung's banner, march on!

COLOMBIA

Words by
RAFAEL NÚÑEZ (1825-1894)

Music by
ORESTE SINDICI (1837-1904)

This anthem was sung for the first time c. 1905. Rafael Núñez was elected President of Colombia four times.

-pren - de las pa-la - bras Del que murió en la Cruz.

2. *INDEPENDENCIA grita*
    El mundo americano;
    Se baña en sangre de héroes
    La tierra de Colón.
    Pero este gran principio:
    EL REY NO ES SOBERANO,
    Resuena, y los que sufren
    Bendicen su pasión.

Translation

CHORUS

Oh unfading glory!
Oh immortal joy!
In furrows of pain
Good is already germinating.

1. The fearful night came to an end,
    Liberty sublime
    Is spreading the dawns
    Of its invincible light.
    The whole of humanity,
    Which is groaning under chains,
    Understands the words
    Of the One who died on the Cross.

2. INDEPENDENCE cries
    The American world;
    In heroes' blood is bathing
    The Land of Columbus.
    But this great principle:
    THE KING IS NOT SOVEREIGN,
    Resounds, and those who suffer
    Praise the passion in it.

COMORO ISLANDS
Udzima wa ya Masiwa
(The Union of the Great Islands)

Words by
SAID HACHIM SIDI ABDEREMANE (b.1942)

Music by
KAMILDINE ABDALLAH (1943-1982) and
SAID HACHIM SIDI ABDEREMANE (b. 1942)
Arr. by W.L. REED

[Con spirito]

I bera - mu i - si pe - pe - za i na - di ukom-bo-zi pi-
mu i - si pe - pe - za ra - ngu mwesi si - ta wa Zui-

ya i dau - la i-ve-nu-ha ta-
ye i dau - la i-ve-nu-ha zi

si - ba bu___ ya i di - ni vo - ya tra-nga-
si - wa za-tru zi pa-ngwi ha Ma-o-re na Nzu-a-

Adopted in 1978.

English Translation by Jan Knappert

The flag is flying,
announcing complete independence;
The nation rises up
because of the faith we have
in this our Comoria.

Let us always have devotion
to love our Great Islands.
We Comorians are of one blood,
We Comorians are of one faith.

On these islands we were born,
These islands brought us up.
May God always help us;
Let us always have the firm resolve
to love our fatherland,
love our religion and the world.

The flag is flying
from the Sixth of July;
The Nation rises up;
Our islands are lined up.
Maori and Anzuan, Moheli and Comore,
Let us always have devotion
to love our Great Islands.

French Translation

Au faîte le Drapeau flotte
Appelle a là Liberté totale.
La nation apparaît,
Force d'une même réligion au sein des COMORES.
Vivons dans l'amour réciproque dans nos îles.

Les Comoriens issue de même sang,
Nous embrassons la même idéologie réligieuse.
Les îles où nous sommes nés!!
Les îles qui nous ont prodigués la bonne éducation.
Dieu y a apporté son aide.
Conservons notre unité pour l'amour de la patrie,
Amour pour la réligion
Et pour l'évolution.

Au faîte le Drapeau flotte
Depuis le 6 du mois de Juillet
La nation apparaît,
Les îles devenues souveraines;
MAORE — N'DZOUANI — MOUWALI — et N'GAZIDJA.
Gardons notre amour pour les îles.

CONGO
Les Trois Glorieuses

Words by
HENRI LOPES (*b.* 1937)

Music by
PHILIPPE MOCKOUAMY (*b.* 1938)
Arranged from band score by
W.L. REED

1. Lè - ve toi, Pa - trie cou - ra - geuse, Toi qui en trois jour - nées glo - ri - euses Sai - sis et por - te le dra - peau Pour un Con - go libre et nou - veau, Qui

Adopted in 1969.

122

ja - mais plus ne fail - li - ra, Que ___ per - sonne n'ef-

fra - ye - ra.

CHORUS

Nous a - vons bri - sé nos chaines, Nous tra-

vail - ler - ons sans ___ peine, Nous sommes une Na-

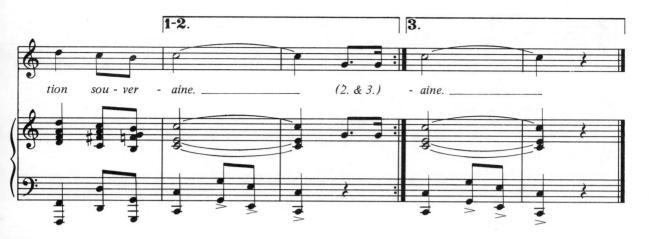

tion   sou - ver - aine. _____ (2. & 3.)   - aine. _____

2. *Si trop tôt me tue l'ennemi,*
   Brave camarade, saisis mon fusil;
   Et si la balle touche mon coeur,
   Toutes nos soeurs se lèveront sans peur,
   Et nos monts, nos flots en fureur
   Repousseront i'envahisseur.

   CHORUS

3. *Ici commence la Patrie*
   Où chaque humain a le même prix.
   Notre seule guide c'est le Peuple.
   Notre génie c'est encore le Peuple.
   C'est lui seul qui a décidé
   De rétablir sa dignité.

   CHORUS

Translation by T.M. Cartledge

1. Arise, brave Fatherland,
   You who in three glorious days
   Seize and carry the banner
   For a new and free Congo
   That will never again fail
   And that no-one will alarm.

   CHORUS   We have broken our chains,
            We shall work untiringly,
            We are a sovereign nation.

2. If the enemy kills me before my time,
   Take my rifle, brave comrade;
   And if the bullet reaches my heart,
   All our sisters will arise fearlessly
   And our mountains and torrents
   Will in anger turn back the invader.

   CHORUS

3. The Fatherland begins here
   Where everyone has the same value.
   Our only guide is the people,
   Our genius too is the people.
   It is the people alone who decided
   To re-establish their dignity.

   CHORUS

COSTA RICA

Words by
JOSÉ MARÍA ZELEDÓN BRENES (1877-1949)
English verses by
MARY ELIZABETH and DICCON SHAW

Music by
MANUEL MARÍA GUTIÉRREZ (1829-1887)

Allegro Marcial

Noble pa - tria tu hermo - sa ban-de - ra   ex - pre-
No - ble coun - try, the life   of your peo - ple   Is re-

- sión de tu vi - da nos da: ba-jo el lim - pi-do a-zul de tu
- veal'd   in the flag that you fly;   For in peace, white and pure, they live

Adopted as the National Anthem in 1853, when composed.
The first two verses allude to the national flag, of which the colours are blue, white and red.
They were chosen as the result of a public competition in 1900.

CUBA
La Bayamesa

Versified by
MARTIN SHAW

Words and music by
PEDRO FIGUEREDO (1819-1870)

Al com - ba - te co - rred, ba - ya-
Swift, oh men of Ba - ya - mo, to

Sung for the first time in 1868 during the battle of Bayamo, in which Figueredo played a leading part.
By permission of J.B. Cramer & Co. Ltd.

CYPRUS

Words by
DIONYSIOS SOLOMÓS (1798-1857)
English versification by
T.M. CARTLEDGE

Music by
NIKOLAOS MANTZAROS (1795-1873)

It was adopted when the Republic of Cyprus achieved independence in 1960.
The National Anthem of Cyprus is the same as that of Greece.

prawt' an three - o - me - nee hye - r'o hye r'e-lef - the -
an - cient val - our ris - ing, Let us hail you, Li - ber-

-rya, _____ Ke san prawt' an three - o -
-ty, _____ Now, with an - cient val - our

-me - nee hye - r'o hye r'e-lef - the - rya. _____
ris - ing, Let us hail you, Li - ber - ty! _____

CZECHOSLOVAKIA
Part 1: Kde Domov Můj?

Words by
JOSEF KAJETÁN TYL (1808-1856)

Music by
FRANTIŠEK SAN ŠKROUP (1801-1862)

This State hymn was officially recognised as the National Anthem in 1919.
It is in two parts. The first is Czech and the second is a Slovak folksong
commemorating the exodus of Slovak students from Bratislava in 1843.

ráj____ to na po-hled! A to je ta krá - sná ze - mě, ze-mě

če - ská do-mov můj, ___ ze-mě če - ská do-mov můj!

Part 2: Nad Tatrú sa blýská

Words by
JANKO MATÚŠKA (1821-1877)

Composer unknown

Allegro energico

Nad Ta - trú sa blý - ská, hro - my di - vo bi - jú,

nad Ta - trú sa blý - ská, hro - my di - vo bi - jú.

Translation

Part 1

Where is my home, where is my home?
Streams are rushing through the meadows,
'Mid the rocks sigh fragrant pine groves,
Orchards decked in Spring's array
Scenes of Paradise portray.
And this land of wond'rous beauty
Is the Czech land, home of mine,
Is the Czech land, home of mine.

Part 2

Lightning strikes our mighty Tatra tempest-shaken,
Lightning strikes our mighty Tatra tempest-shaken.
Stand we fast, friends of mine,
Storms must pass, sun will shine,
Slovaks shall awaken.

DENMARK
Kong Kristian

Words by
JOHANNES EWALD (1743-1781)
English versification by
HENRY WADSWORTH LONGFELLOW (1807-1882)

Music by
DITLEV LUDVIG ROGERT (1742-1813)
This is not certain.

This is the official National and Royal Anthem. Music first appeared in manuscript form c. 1762-1777; words first used in the ballad opera *The Fishermen* 1780. There are other verses.
* King Christian IV (1577-1648) was one of Denmark's great patriotic leaders.

spejl og— mast I røg og damp. "Fly," skreg de, "fly, hvad
hulk and mast In mist and smoke. "Fly!" shout-ed they, "fly,

flyg - te kan! Hvo står for Dan - marks Kri - sti - an, Hvo
he who can! Who braves of Den - mark's Christ - i - an, Who

står for Dan - marks Kri - sti - an i kamp?"
braves of Den - mark's Christ-i - an The stroke?"

DJIBOUTI

Words by
ADEN ELMI (*b.* 1950)

Music by
ABDI ROBLEH (*b.* 1945)
Arr. by W.L. REED

Officially adopted in 1977.

Hinjinne u sara kaca
Calankaan harraad iyo
Haydaar u mudateen.

Hir cagaarku qariyayiyo
Habkay samadu tahayoo
Xiddig dhi igleh hoorshoo
Caddaan lagu hadheeyaay.

Maxaa haybad kugu yaal.

Free Translation

Arise with strength; for we have raised our flag,
The flag which has cost us dear
With extremes of thirst and pain.

Our flag, whose colours are the everlasting green of the earth,
The blue of the sky, and white, the colour of peace;
And in the centre the red star of blood.

Oh flag of ours, what a glorious sight!

DOMINICA

Words by
WILFRED OSCAR MORGAN POND (*b.* 1912)

Music by
LEMUEL McPHERSON CHRISTIAN (*b.* 1913)
Arr. by W.L. REED

Originally adopted in 1967 on achieving Statehood and again in 1978 when becoming independent.

DOMINICAN REPUBLIC

Words by
EMILIO PRUD'HOMME (1856-1932)
English versification by
J.E. HALES and
MARY ELIZABETH SHAW

Music by
JOSÉ REYÉS (1835-1905)

First sung as National Anthem in 1900. Quisqueya is the native name of the island of Santo Domingo.
By permission of J.B. Cramer & Co. Ltd.

mun - do a la faz os - ten - te - mos nues-tro in-vic - to glo - rio - so pen-
-fi - ant and daunt-less, be - fore us We will flou - rish our stan - dard un-

- dón. ¡Sal - ve el pue - blo que in tré - pi - do y fuer - te, a la
furled. Hail! O peo - ple in - tre - pid and dar - ing, Who with

gue - rra a mo - rir se lan - zó. Cuan-do en bé - li - co re - to de
ea - ger - ness sprang to at - tack; And, of blood-shed and dan - ger un-

muer - te sus ca - de - nas de es - cla - vo rom-
-car - ing, Saw the fet - ters of sla - ve - ry

-pló el he - ro - is - mo vi - ril. Mas Quis-que - ya la in-dó - mi - tá y
true vi - rile cour - age de - rives. But the sons of Quis - que - ya ne'er

bra - va Siem-pre al - ti - va la fren - te al - za -
fail her, And her head car - ried high shall re -

-rá: Que si fue - re mil ve - ces es -
-main; Though a thou - sand times foes should as -

-cla - va O - tras tan - tas ser li - bre sa - brá.
-sail her, She her free - dom would e - ver re - gain.

ECUADOR

Words by
JUAN LEÓN MERA (1832-1894)
English versification by
T.M. CARTLEDGE

Music by
ANTONIO NEUMANE (1818-1871)

Officially recognised as the National Anthem by a government decree in 1948. It had been in use for a considerable time before. The author, in his later years, was President of the Senate of Ecuador.

VERSE

Los pri-mo-ros los hi-jos del sue-lo que so-
Com-ing first were the sons of the coun-try Which Pi-

-ber-bio, el Pi-chin-cha de-co - ra Te a-cla-
-chin-cha on high is a-dorn - ing, Who ac-

-ma - ron por siem-pre se - ño - ra Y ver-
-claimed you as their sov' - reign la - dy And shed-

-tie - ron su san-gre por ti Dios mi-
blood for the sake of the land: God look'd

ró y a-cep-tó el ho-lo-ca - us-to Ye-sa,
on and ac-cept - ed the sa - cri-fice, And that

san - gre fue ger-men fe-cun - do De o-tros
blood was seed pro-li - fic; Oth - er

hé - roes que a-tó - ni-to el mun - do Vió en tu
her - oes the world ob-served, as-tound - ed, For the

EGYPT

Words and music by
SAYED DARWISH (1892-1923)
Arr. by W.L. REED

Allegretto maestoso (♩ = 96)
CHORUS

Bi -la - di bi -la - di___ bi -la - - di La - ki

hu - bbi ___ wa fu - a - - di ___ Bi - la - di bi -

la - di bi - la - - - di La - ki hu - bbi ___ wa fu -

Adopted in 1979.

D.S. al Fine

Fine VERSES

di La - ki hu - bbi _____ wa fu - a - - - di

pp

{ 2. Mis - r }
{ 3. Mis - r }

pp

2. Misr inti aghla durra
   Fawq gabeen ad-dahr ghurra
   Ya biladi 'aishi hurra
   Wa as'adi raghm-al-adi.

CHORUS. Biladi etc.

3. Misr awladik kiram
   Aufiya yar'u-zimam
   Saufa takhti bil-maram
   Bittihadhim wa-ittihadi.

CHORUS. Biladi etc.

Translation

CHORUS. My homeland, my homeland, my homeland,
         My love and my heart are for thee.
         My homeland, my homeland, my homeland,
         My love and my heart are for thee.

1. Egypt! O mother of all lands,
   My hope and my ambition,
   How can one count
   The blessings of the Nile for mankind?

CHORUS. My homeland, etc.

2. Egypt! Most precious jewel,
   Shining on the brow of eternity!
   O my homeland, be for ever free,
   Safe from every foe!

CHORUS. My homeland, etc.

3. Egypt! Noble are thy children,
   Loyal, and guardians of thy soil.
   In war and peace
   We give our lives for thy sake.

CHORUS. My homeland, etc.

EL SALVADOR

Words by
JUAN JOSÉ CAÑAS (1826-1918)
English versification by
MARY ELIZABETH SHAW
and DICCON SHAW

Music by
JUAN ABERLE (1846-1930)

This was written in 1879 and adopted as the National Anthem in 1953.
General Juan Cañas was a diplomat and soldier; at one time Minister of Foreign Affairs.
English words copyright J.B. Cramer & Co. Ltd.

su - yos po - der - nos lla - mar_____ Y ju -
name_____ of thy chil - dren we bear,_____ And with

- re - mos la vi - da a - ni - mo - sos Sin des -
bold and un - tir - ing de - vo - tion To thy_____

can - so a su bien con - sa - grar.
ser - vice our lives let us swear.

f

Sa - lu -
Moth - er

I

-de - mos la Pa - tria or - gu - llo - sos De hi - jos
coun - try, thy peo - ple sa - lute thee! Proud - ly the

su - llos po-der - nos lla - mar___ Y ju -
name___ of thy chil - dren we bear,___ And with

-re - mos la vi - da a - ni - mo - sos Sin des
bold and un-tir - ing de - vo - tion to thy___

-can - so a su bien___ con - sa - grar
ser - vice our lives___ let us swear.

- gre - so se a-fa - na en se-guir en se-guir Por lle-
bright star of pro - gress she fol - lows the way; To se -

- nar___ su gran-dio - so des - ti - no, _____ Con - quis-
- cure___ for her-self a hap - py fu - ture, _____ And her

- tar___ se un fe - liz___ por - ve - nir Le pro-
des - ti - ny glo - rious o - bey. The at -

- te - - - je u-na fè - rrea ba - rre - ra Con tra el
- tack _____ of a vil - lain - ous trai - tor Her___

cho - - - que de ruin des-leal - tad   Des - de el
ram - - - part of steel has with-stood   Since the

dí - - - a que en su alta ban - de - - ra Con su
day_____ when a-loft on her stan - - dard She wrote the

san - gre es-cri-bió_____ li-ber-tad!____ es-cri-bió_____ li-ber-
"Free - dom" in let - ters of blood,____ She wrote "Free - dom" in

tad!____ es-cri-bió_____ li-ber-tad!
let - ters, in let - ters of blood.

D.C. al Fine

D.C. al Fine

CORO   *Saludemos la patria orgullosos*
De Hijos suyos podernos llamar;
Y juremos la vida animosos,
Sin descanso a su bien consagrar.

2.   *Libertad es su dogma, es su guia,*
Que mil veces logró defender;
Y otras tantas de audaz tirania
Rechazar el odioso poder.
     Dolorosa y sangrienta es su historia,
Pero excelsa y brillante a la vez,
Manantial de legitima gloria,
Gran lección de espartana altivez.
     No desmaya su innata bravura:
En cada hombre hay un héroe inmortal,
Que sabrá mantenerse a la altura
De su antiguo valor proverbial.

3.   *Todos son abnegados y fieles*
Al prestigio del bélico ardor,
Con que siempre segaron laureles
De la Patria salvando el honor.
     Respetar los derechos extraños
Y apoyarse en la recta razón
Es para ella, sin torpes amaños,
La invariable, más firme ambición.
     Y en seguir esta linea se aferra,
Dedicando su esfuerzo tenaz
En hacer cruda guerra a la guerra;
Su ventura se encuentra en la paz.

CHORUS   Mother country, thy people salute thee!
Proudly the name of thy children we bear,
And with bold and untiring devotion
To thy service our lives let us swear.

2.   Never tiring, her people have battled
To preserve and guard their liberty:
And with valour have a thousand times over
Broken the powers of base tyranny.
For, though brilliant and sublime is her story,
Yet it tells of her blood and her suffering beside,
And in this is revealed her true glory
And her noble and stoical pride.
All her sons shall be heroes immortal;
They are daring, resourceful, and bold;
For their bravery is a tradition
And they fight like their fathers of old.

3.   They will follow this ancient tradition
Which has won for them undying fame,
Since with ardour, self-denying and faithful,
They kept spotless their Motherland's name.
Her ambition is firm and unchanging,
To respect and observe others' rights is her pride;
To maintain ever pure the fount of justice
Where uprightness and trust are allied.
She will follow this path with devotion
And with courage which never shall cease;
For, although she gives battle for battle,
Her most fervent desire is for peace.

EQUATORIAL GUINEA

Words by
ATANASIO NDONGO MIYONO* (*d.* 1969)

Music
Arr. by W.L. REED

* Date of birth unknown.
Adopted in 1968, year of independence.
Words not yet available.

ETHIOPIA

Words by
ASSEFA GEBRE-MARIAM TESSAMA (*b.* 1936)

Music by
DANIEL YOHANNES HAGGOS (*b.* 1950)
Arranged and harmonised by
W.L. REED

First used on Revolution Day, 1 September, 1975.

Transliteration and translation by D.L. Appleyard

Ethiopia, Ethiopia — Ethiopia, be first
In socialism — flourish, be fertile!

Your brave sons have made a covenant,
That your rivers and mountains, your virgin land
Should be a sacrifice for the unity of Ethiopia, for your freedom,
To your honour and renown!

Strive forwards on the road of wisdom,
Gird yourself for the task,
For the prosperity of the land!

You are the mother of heroes — be proud of your sons,
May your enemies perish — may you live for ever!

FIJI

Words by
MICHAEL FRANCIS ALEXANDER PRESCOTT (*b.* 1928)

Composer unknown
Harmonisation as used by
Royal Fiji Police Band

1. Bless - ing grant, oh God of na - tions, on the isles of Fi - ji,
2. Bless - ing grant, oh God of na - tions, on the isles of Fi - ji,

As we stand u - ni - ted un - der no - ble ban - ner blue.
Shores of gold - en sand and sun - shine, hap - pi - ness and song.

And we hon - our and de - fend the cause of free - dom ev - er,
Stand u - ni - ted, we of Fi - ji, fame and glo - ry ev - er,

CHORUS

On - ward march to - geth - er, God bless Fi - ji!
On - ward march to - geth - er, God bless Fi - ji! For

Fiji became an independent Commonwealth country on the 10 October, 1970.

Fi - ji,   ev - er Fi—ji,   let our voi - ces ring with pride,   For

Fi - ji,   ev - er Fi - ji,   her name hail far and   wide, A land of

free - dom,   hope and glo - ry   to en - dure what - e'er be - fall. May God bless

D.C.

Fi - ji,   for ev - er - more!_____

FINLAND
Maamme Laulu
(Our Land)

Words by
JOHAN LUDVIG RUNEBERG (1804-1877)
Translation by
CHARLES WHARTON STORK

Music by
FREDRIK PACIUS (1809-1891)

This anthem was written by Finland's National Poet in 1846.
Sung for the first time at a students' gathering, 13 May, 1848.

vet - tä, ran - taa__ rak-kaam-paa, Kuin ko - ti-maa tää poh-joi-
gen - tle dales or__ foam-ing strand Are loved as we our home re-

- nen, Maa kal - lis i - si - eñ!
-vere, The earth our sires held dear.

2. *Sun kukoistukses kuorestaan*
Kerrankin puhkeaa!
Viel' lempemme saa nousemaan
Sun toivos, riemus loistossaan,
Ja kerran laulus, synnyinmaa,
Korkeemman kaiun saa!

2. The flowers in their buds that grope
Shall burst their sheaths with spring;
So from our love to bloom shall ope
Thy gleam, thy glow, thy joy, thy hope,
And higher yet some day shall ring
The patriot song we sing!

FRANCE
La Marseillaise

English translation of first verse by
PERCY BYSSHE SHELLEY (1792-1822)
of second verse by
MARY ELIZABETH SHAW

Words and music by
CLAUDE-JOSEPH ROUGET de L'ISLE (1760-1836)

1. *Al-lons en-fants de la Pa-tri- e, Le jour de gloire est ar-ri-vé. Con-tre nous, de la ty-ran-ni- e, L'é-ten-dard sang-lant est le-vé, l'é-ten-*

1. Ye sons of France, a-wake to glo-ry, Hark, hark, what my-riads bid you rise: Your child-ren, wives and grand-sires hoa-ry, *See their tears and hear their cries, see their*

*Shelley has "behold"

Written and composed on 24 April, 1792, as a marching song.
Adopted as National Anthem, 15 July, 1795.

-mez ___ vos ba-tail-lons, ___ Mar- chons, mar- chons!
-veng - ing sword un-sheathe! ___ March on! march on!

Qu'un sang im - pur ___ A - breu - ve nos sil-lons.
All hearts re - solved ___ on vic - to-ry or death.

2. *Amour sacré de la Patrie,*
    Conduis, soutiens nos bras vengeurs.
    Liberté, liberté chérie,
    Combats avec tes défenseurs; (bis)
    Sous nos drapeaux, que la victoire
    Accoure à tes mâles accents;
    Que tes ennemis expirants
    Voient ton triomphe et notre gloire!

    ˣAux armes citoyens, etc.

2. O sacred love of France, undying,
    Th'avenging arm uphold and guide.
    Thy defenders, death defying,
    Fight with Freedom at their side.
    Soon thy sons shall be victorious
    When the banner high is raised;
    And thy dying enemies, amazed,
    Shall behold thy triumph, great and glorious.

    To arms, to arms, ye brave! etc.

* It is customary to repeat *'Aux armes citoyens'*

GABON

Words and music by
GEORGES DAMAS ALEKA (*b.* 1902)
Arr. by HENRY COLEMAN

Tempo di Marcia

U - ni _____ dans la Con-cor - de et la _____ fra-ter-ni-té, _____ E - veil-le-toi Ga-bon, une au - ro - re se lè - ve, En-cou-ra-ge l'ar-deur qui

This became the National Anthem upon independence on 17 August, 1960.

178

2. *Oui que le temps heureux rêvé par nos ancêtres*
   Arrive enfin chez nous, rejouisse les êtres,
   Et chasse les sorciers, ces perfides trompeurs
   Qui semaient le poison et répandaient la peur.

3. *Afin qu'aux yeux du monde et des nations amies*
   Le Gabon immortel reste digne d'envie,
   Oublions nos querelles, ensemble bâtissons
   L'édifice nouveau auquel tous nous rêvons.

4. *Des bords de l'Ocean au cœur de la forêt,*
   Demeurons vigilants, sans faiblesse et sans haine!
   Autour de ce drapeau, qui vers l'honneur nous mène,
   Saluons la Patrie et chantons sans arrêt:

Translation by
T.M. Cartledge

Chorus   United in concord and brotherhood,
Awake, Gabon, dawn is at hand.
Stir up the spirit that thrills and inspires us!
At last we rise up to attain happiness.

1. Dazzling and proud, the sublime day dawns,
   Dispelling for ever injustice and shame.
   May it still advance and calm our fears,
   May it promote virtue and banish warfare.

2. Yes, may the happy days of which our ancestors dreamed
   Come for us at last, rejoicing our hearts,
   And banish the sorcerers, those perfidious deceivers
   Who sowed poison and spread fear.

3. So that, in the eyes of the world and of friendly nations,
   The immortal Gabon may maintain her good repute,
   Let us forget our quarrels, let us build together
   The new structure of which we all have dreamed.

4. From the shores of the Ocean to the heart of the forest,
   Let us remain vigilant, without weakness and without hatred!
   Around this flag which leads us to honour,
   Let us salute the Fatherland and ever sing:

THE GAMBIA

Words by
VIRGINIA JULIA HOWE (*b.* 1927)

Adapted by **JEREMY FREDERIC HOWE** (*b.* 1929)
from the traditional Mandinka song
"Foday Kaba Dumbuya"

For the Gam - bi - a, our__ home - land, We__ strive and work and pray, That all may__ live in u - ni - ty, Free - dom and peace each day. Let jus - tice guide our ac - tions To -

Copyright by Government of The Gambia.
Officially adopted 18 February, 1965, when the country became independent.

GERMANY
Democratic Republic

Words by
JOHANNES ROBERT BECHER (1891-1958)
English words by
YVONNE KAPP

Music by
HANNS EISLER (1898-1962)

Moderato

1. Auf - er - stan - den aus Ru - i - nen Und der Zu - kunft
1. From the ru - ins ris - en new - ly To the fu - ture

zu - ge - wandt, Lass uns dir zum Gu - ten die - nen,
turned we stand. May we serve your good weal tru - ly,

Deutsch - land, ei - nig Va - ter - land. _____ Al - te Not gilt
Ger - ma - ny, our moth - er - land. _____ Tri - umph o - ver

Adopted in 1949.
© Edition Peters, Leipzig, East Germany.

es zu zwin - gen,____ Und wir zwin - gen sie ver - eint,
by - gone sor - row____ Can in u - ni - ty be won,

Denn es muss uns doch ge - lin - gen, Dass die Son - ne schön wie
For we must at - tain a mor - row When o - ver our Ger - ma -

nie Ü - ber Deutsch - land scheint, ü - ber Deutsch - land scheint.
ny There is ra - diant sun, there is ra - diant sun.

2.   *Glück und Friede sei beschieden*
     Deutschland, unsrem Vaterland.
     Alle Welt sehnt sich nach Frieden,
     Reicht den Völkern eure Hand.
     Wenn wir Bründerlich uns einen,
     Schlagen wir des Volkes Feind.
     Lasst des Licht des Friedens scheinen,
     Dass nie eine Mutter mehr
     Ihren Sohn beweint, ihren Sohn beweint!

3.   *Lasst uns pflügen, lasst uns bauen,*
     Lernt und schafft wie nie zuvor,
     Und der eigen Kraft vertrauend
     Steigt einfrei Geschlect empor.
     Deutsche Jugend bestes Streben
     Unsres Volks in dir vereint,
     Wirst du Deutschlands neues Leben,
     Und die Sonne schön wie nie
     Über Deutschland scheint, über Deutschland scheint.

2.   May both joy and peace inspire
     Germany, our motherland
     Peace is all the world's desire.
     To the peoples give your hand.
     In fraternity united
     We shall crush the people's foe.
     May our path by peace be lighted
     That no mother shall again
     Mourn her son in woe.

3.   Let us till and build our nation,
     Learn and work as never yet
     That a free new generation
     Faith in its own strength beget
     German youth, for whom the striving
     Of our people is at one,
     You are Germany's reviving
     And over our Germany
     There is radiant sun.

GERMANY
Federal Republic

Words by
AUGUST HEINRICH HOFFMAN von FALLERSLEBEN
(1798-1874)

Music by
FRANZ JOSEPH HAYDN
(1732-1809)

Ein - ig - keit und Recht und Frei - heit für das deut - sche Va - ter - land! Da - nach lasst uns al - le stre - ben brü - der - lich mit Herz und Hand! Ein - ig -

Authorised as National Anthem on 11 August, 1922 when the first verse of von Fallersleben's poem was sung. In 1950 the Federal Republic adopted the third verse instead as the official words.

-keit und Recht und Frei-heit sind des Glück - es Un - ter -
-pfand Blüh im Glan - ze die - ses
Glück - es blü - he__ deut - sches Va - ter - land!

Free Translation

Unity and right and freedom
For the German fatherland;
Let us all pursue the purpose
Brotherly, with heart and hands.
Unity and right and freedom
Are the pawns of happiness.

Bis { Flourish in this blessing's glory,
Flourish, German fatherland!

GHANA

Words by
GHANA GOVERNMENT

Music by
PHILIP GBEHO (1905-1976)

Ritmico, con moto

f

1. God bless our home - land Gha - na __ And make our na - tion
2. Hail to thy name, __ O Gha - na, __ To thee we make our

great and strong, __ Bold to de - fend for __ ev - er __ The
sol - emn vow: __ Stead - fast to build to - geth - er __ A

Right; __

cause of Free - dom and __ of Right; and __ of Right; Fill __ our
na - tion strong __ in U - ni - ty; in U - ni - ty; With __ our

- ty; __

hearts with __ true hu - mil - i - ty, Make us
gifts of __ mind and __ strength of __ arm, Wheth - er

Officially became the National Anthem in 1957, the year when independence was attained. The original words were written in 1956, as was the music, but replaced by the present text following a change of government in 1966.

cher - ish ____ fear - less hon - es - ty, ____ And
night or ____ day, in mist or ____ storm, ____ In

help us to re - sist op - pres - sor's rule With all our
ev - 'ry need, what - e'er the call may be, To serve thee,

will and might for ev - er - more. ____ And more. ____
Gha - na, now_ and ev - er - more. ____ In more. ____

D.C.

3. Raise high the flag of Ghana
   And one with Africa advance;
   Black Star of hope and honour
   To all who thirst for Liberty;
   Where the banner of Ghana freely flies,
   May the way to freedom truly lie;
   Arise, arise, O sons of Ghanaland,
   And under God march on for evermore!

GREAT BRITAIN
God Save The Queen

Author unknown

Composer unknown

Moderato

1. God save our gra - cious Queen, Long live our no - ble Queen,

God save the Queen: Send her vic - to - ri - ous, Hap - py and

glo - ri - ous, Long to — reign o - ver us: God save the Queen.

2. O Lord our God arise,
Scatter her enemies,
And make them fall:
Confound their politics,
Frustrate their knavish tricks,
On Thee our hopes we fix:
God save us all.

3. Thy choicest gifts in store
On her be pleased to pour;
Long may she reign:
May she defend our laws,
And ever give us cause
To sing with heart and voice
God save the Queen.

Earliest copy of words in Gentleman's Magazine, 1745.
The melody is also that of the National Anthem of Liechtenstein.

GREECE

Words by
DIONYSIOS SOLOMÓS (1798-1857)
English versification by
T.M. CARTLEDGE

Music by
NIKOLAOS MANTZAROS (1795-1873)

Chosen as the National Anthem by King George I and adopted in 1864.
There are 158 verses. The National Anthem of Greece is the same as that of Cyprus.

Music copyright J.B. Cramer & Co. Ltd.

prawt' an - three - o - me - nee hye - r'o hye r'e - lef - the -
an - cient val - our ris - ing, Let us hail you, Li - ber -

-rya, _____ Ke san prawt' an three - o -
-ty, _____ Now, with an - cient val - our

-me - nee hye - r'o hye - r'e - lef - the - rya. _____
ris - ing, Let us hail you, Li - ber - ty! _____

GRENADA

Words by
IRVA MERLE BAPTISTE (*b.* 1924)

Music by
LOUIS ARNOLD MASANTO (*b.* 1938)

Hail! Gre-na-da, land of ours, We pledge our-selves to thee, Heads, hearts and hands in u-ni-ty To reach our des-ti-ny. Ev-er

Officially adopted on Independence Day, 7 February, 1974.

194

GUATEMALA

Words by
JOSÉ JOAQUÍN PALMA (1844-1911)
Versified by
MARTIN, MARY ELIZABETH and DICCON SHAW

Music by
RAFAEL ALVAREZ OVALLE (1860-1948)

This was chosen from entries in a public competition in 1887.
Adopted by governmental decrees of 28 October, 1896 and 19 February, 1897, and modified by decree of 26 July, 1934.
By permission of J.B. Cramer & Co. Ltd.

VERSE

¡Gua-te - ma - la fe - liz! que tus a - ras no pro-
Gua-te - ma - la, blest land, home of hap - py race, May thine

-fa - ne ja - más el ver - du - go; ni ha-ya es - cla - vos que la - man el
al - tars pro - fa - ned be nev - er; No yoke of sla - ver-y weigh on thee

yu - go ni ti - ra - nos que es-cu - pan tu faz. Si ma-
e - ver, Nor may ty-rants e'er spit in thy face. Should to-

CHORUS

Li- bre al vien - to tu her - mo - sa ban - de - ra a ven-
Your loved flag to the winds free - ly fly - ing Will

-cer o a mo - rir lla - ma - rá; que tu pue - blo con á - ni - ma
call you to con - quer or die. You would soon - er be slain fight - ing

fie - ra an - tes muer - to q'es - cla - vo se - rá.
brave - ly Than sub - ject - ed in sla - ve - ry lie.

GUINEA
Liberté

Music by
KODOFO MOUSSA

Became independent 2 October, 1958.
Words not yet available.

GUINEA – BISSAU

Words and music by
AMILCAR CABRAL (1924-1973)

1. Sol, su - or e o ver - de e mar, __ Sé - cu-los de dor e es-peran-ça:
2. Ra - mos do mes-mo tron-co, Ol - hos na mes-ma luz:

Es - ta é a ter - ra dos nos - sos a-vós! Fru - to das nos - sas mãos,
Es - ta é a for - ça da nos - sa u-nião! Can - tem o mar e a ter - ra

Composed in 1963.
Adopted as the National Anthem on Independence Day, 24 September, 1974.

Translation

1. Sun, sweat, verdure and sea,
   Centuries of pain and hope;
   This is the land of our ancestors.
   Fruit of our hands,
   Of the flower of our blood:
   This is our beloved country.

2. Branches of the same trunk,
   Eyes in the same light;
   This is the force of our unity!
   The sea and the land,
   The dawn and the sun are singing
   That our struggle has borne fruit!

Chorus   Long live our glorious country!
           The banner of our struggle
           Has fluttered in the skies.
           Forward, against the foreign yoke!
           We are going to build
           Peace and progress
           In our immortal country!

GUYANA

Words by
ARCHIBALD LEONARD LUKER
(1917-1971)

Music by
ROBERT CYRIL GLADSTONE POTTER
(1899-1981)

The words and music were selected as the result of a competition. This anthem was approved by the House of Assembly on 21 April, 1966. The country became independent 26 May, 1966.

204

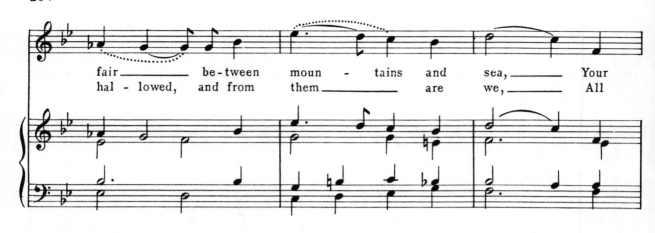

3. Great land of Guyana, diverse though our strains,
   We are born of their sacrifice, heirs of their pains,
   And ours is the glory their eyes did not see –
   One land of six peoples, united and free.

4. Dear land of Guyana, to you will we give
   Our homage, our service, each day that we live;
   God guard you, great Mother, and make us to be
   More worthy our heritage – land of the free.

HAITI
La Dessalinienne

Words by
JUSTIN LHÉRISSON (1873-1907)
English versification by
MARTIN SHAW
First verse by
MARY ELIZABETH SHAW and DICCON SHAW

Music by
NICOLAS GEFFRARD (1871-1930)

This anthem was composed for the centenary of national independence in 1904. The title is derived from Jean-Jacques Dessalines, the founder of Haiti as an independent republic, of which he crowned himself Emperor.

English words copyright J.B. Cramer & Co. Ltd.

2. *Pour les Aïeux*
    Pour la Patrie
    Bêchons joyeux:
    Quand le champ fructifie
    L'âme se fortifie
    Bêchons joyeux
    Pour les Aïeux,
    Pour la Patrie.

3. *Pour le Pays*
    Et pour nos Pères
    Formons des Fils.
    Libres, forts et prospères,
    Toujours: nous serons frères,
    Formons des fils
    Pour le Pays
    Et pour nos Pères.

4. *Pour les Aïeux*
    Pour la Patrie
    O Dieu des Preux!
    Sous ta garde infinie
    Prends nos droits, notre vie,
    O Dieu des Preux!
    Pour les Aïeux,
    Pour la Patrie.

5. *Pour le Drapeau*
    Pour la Patrie,
    Mourir est beau!
    Notre passé nous crie:
    Ayez l'âme aguerrie!
    Mourir est beau
    Pour le Drapeau,
    Pour la Patrie.

2. For sacred soil,
    For sires of old
    We gladly toil.
    When teem field and wold
    The soul is strong and bold.
    We gladly toil, we gladly toil
    For sacred soil,
    For sires of old.

3. For land we love
    And sires of old
    We give our sons.
    Free, happy, and bold,
    One brotherhood we'll hold.
    We give our sons, we give our sons
    For land we love
    And sires of old.

4. For those who gave
    For country all,
    God of the brave,
    To Thee, O God, we call;
    Without Thee we must fall,
    God of the brave, God of the brave.
    For those who gave
    For country all.

5. For flag on high
    For Native land
    'Tis fine to die.
    Our traditions demand
    Be ready, heart and hand,
    'Tis fine to die, 'tis fine to die
    For flag on high,
    For Native land.

HONDURAS

Words by
AUGUSTO CONSTANCIO COELLO (1883-1941)
English versification by
J.E. HALES
(From the translation by
TIBURCIO CARIAS)

Music by
CARLOS HARTLING (1869-1920)

Tu ban-de - ra, tu ban-de - ra es un
As your stan - dard, as your stan - - dard serves a

lam - po de cie - lo   por un blo - - que, por un
strip of cloud-less a - zure,   Which in twain   is cut, which in

blo - - que de_ nie - ve cru - za - do;   y se
twain   is cut by a band that snows be-sprin - kle;   In whose

This anthem was selected as a result of a public competition. It was adopted as the National Anthem in 1915.

By permission of J.B. Cramer & Co. Ltd.

210

2. *Por guardar ese emblema divino,*
marcharemos Oh Patria a la muerte,
generosa será nuestra suerte,
si morimos pensando en tu amor.—
Defendiendo tu santa bandera
y en tus pliegues gloriosos cubiertos,
serán muchos, Oh Honduras tus muertos,
pero todos caerán con honor.—

2. In defence of our glorious emblem
We are ready, my Country, to perish,
For future ages their fame will ever cherish
Who in their dying hour are thinking of your love.
In the defence of your holy banner fallen,
Their lifeless forms in its hallowed folds enshrouded.
Not few, blessed Honduras, shall be your proud dead,
But they all in honour's cause will die.

HUNGARY

Words by
FERENC KÖLCSEY (1790-1838)

Music by
FERENC ERKEL (1810-1893)
Arr. by HENRY COLEMAN

Is - ten áldd meg a ma - gyart *Jó kedv - vel bő - ség - gel. Nyújts fe - lè - je vé - dő kart,*
God bless the Hun - gar - i - ans, Give them joy and plen - ty, Pro - tect their bat - tal - i - ons

Ferenc Erkel was the creator of the Hungarian romantic Grand Opera. From 1875-1886 he was Director of the National Academy of Music, and he founded in 1867 the National Association of Hungarian Choirs.

This was awarded first prize in a national competition in 1844 when it was officially adopted.

ICELAND
Lofsöngur

Words by
MATTHÍAS JOCHUMSSON (1835-1920)

Music by
SVEINBJÖRN SVEINBJÖRNSSON (1847-1926)

Written and composed in 1874, when Iceland secured its own constitution and also celebrated the one thousandth anniversary of the first permanent settlers of Europeans (Norwegians) on the island.

Translation by Jakobina Johnson

Our country's God! Our country's God!
We worship Thy name in its wonder sublime.
The suns of the heavens are set in Thy crown
By Thy legions, the ages of time!
With Thee is each day as a thousand years,
Each thousand of years, but a day,
Eternity's flower with its homage of tears,
That reverently passes away.
    Iceland's thousand years! *(repeat)*
Eternity's flower with its homage of tears,
That reverently passes away.

INDIA
Jană Gană Mană

Words and music by
RABINDRANATH TAGORE (1861-1941)*
Arr. by BRYSON GERRARD

Maestoso

Jană gană mană ad-hi - ña-ya-ka ja-yă hé! Bhā - ra-tă bha-gyă vi-dhā - tā. Pan - jā - bă, Sin - dhă, Guj-rā - tă, Ma - hā - rā - ta, Dra - vi-dă, Ut - ka-lă, Van - gă, Vind-hyă, Hi - mā - cha-lă,

Officially adopted by the Constitutional Assembly on 24 January, 1950, two days before the proclamation of the Republic.

First published 1912, it was for some years prior to adoption associated with India's struggle for independence.

* Rabindranath Tagore also wrote the words and music of the National Anthem of Bangladesh.

*See Footnote 2 (Page 221)

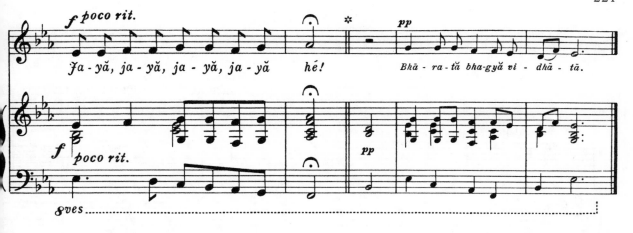

Ja - yǎ, ja - yǎ, ja - yǎ, ja - yǎ hé! Bhā - ra - tǎ bha-gyǎ vi - dhā - tǎ.

Free Translation

Thou art the ruler of the minds
    of all people,
Thou Dispenser of India's destiny,
Thy name rouses the hearts
    of the Punjab, Sind,
      Gujrat and Maratha, of Dravid,
      Orissa and Bengal.
It echoes in the hills of
    the Vindhyas and Himalayas,
    Mingles in the music of
    Jumna and Ganges,
    and is chanted by the waves
    of the Indian sea.
They pray for Thy blessing
    and sing Thy praise,
Thou Dispenser of India's destiny,
Victory, Victory, Victory to Thee!

*Note 1. It will be noticed that the tune ends on the subdominant. The two bars in small notes at the end are not infrequently added — but they are not part of the original melody.

   2. For ordinary performances it is usual to end at the first asterisk.

INDONESIA

Words and music by
WAGE RUDOLF SUPRATMAN (1903-1938)

1. In - do - ne - sia___ ta-nah a-ir ku Ta-nah tum-pah da - rah - ku. Di - sa-
2. In - do - ne - sia!___ Ta-nah jang mu - lia, Ta-nah ki - ta jang ka - ja. Di - sa-
3. In - do - ne - sia!___ Ta-nah jang su - tji, Ta-nah ki - ta jang sak - ti. Di - sa-

This was adopted as the Nationalist Party Song in 1928, and became the National Anthem in 1949.

224

Free Translation

1. INDONESIA, our native country,
   Consecrated with our spilt blood,
   Where we all arise to stand guard
   Over this our Motherland:
   Indonesia our nationality,
   Our people and our country.
   Come then, let us all demand
   Indonesia united.
   Long live our land,
   Long live our state,
   Our nation, our people, and all
   Arouse then its spirit,
   Organise its own bodies
   To obtain Indonesia the Great.

2. INDONESIA, an eminent country,
   Our wealthy country,
   There we shall be forever.
   Indonesia, the country of our
   ancestors,
   A relic of all of us.
   Let us pray
   For Indonesia's prosperity:
   May her soil be fertile
   And spirited her soul,
   The nation and all the people.
   Conscious be her heart
   And her mind
   For Indonesia the Great.

3. INDONESIA, a sacred country,
   Our victorious country:
   There we stand
   Guarding our true Mother.
   Indonesia, a beaming Country,
   A country we love with all our heart,
   Let's make a vow
   That Indonesia be there forever.
   Blessed be her people
   And her sons,
   All her islands, and her seas.
   Fast be the country's progress
   And the progress of her youth
   For Indonesia the Great.

CHORUS   INDONESIA the Great, independent and free,
         My beloved land and country.
         Indonesia the Great, independent and free,
         Long live Indonesia the Great!

IRAN

Words by
ABOLGHASEM HALAT

Music by
MOHAMMAD BEGLARY
Arr. by W.L. REED

March tempo (♩ = 120)

1. Shod jom - hoo - ree - ye es - lah - me be - pah, Ke
2. Ah - zah - dee cho gol - hah dar khah - ke mah She -

ham deen de - had ham don - yah be - mah.
kof - te shod az khoo - ne pah - ke mah.

Az en - qe - lah - be Ee - ran de - gar
Ee - rahn fe - re - stad bah een so - rood

This replaced the Imperial Anthem on 24 March, 1980.

Kah - khe se - tam gash - te zeer - o - ze - bar.
Raz - man - de - gah - ne va - tan - rah do - rood.

Tas - vee - re ah - yan - de - ye mah
Ah - yee - ne jom - hoo - ree ye mah

marc.

Naq - she mo - rah - de mahst.
Posht va pa - nah - he mahst.

Nee - roo - ye pah - yan - de -
Soo - de sa - lah - shoo - re -

ye mah
ye mah

Ee - mahn va et - te - hah - de
Ah - zah - dee va re - fah - he

Translation

1. The Islamic Republic has been established,
   Giving us both the Faith and the World.
   Through the Iranian Revolution
   The palace of oppression has been overturned.
   The image of our future
   Is the role of our desire.
   Our enduring power
   Is our faith and unity.
   Our helper is the hand of God.
   He is our guide in this battle.
   Under the shadow of the Qor'an
   May Iran be permanent, everlasting!

2. Liberty has blossomed from our pure blood
   Like the flowers in our soil.
   Through this hymn Iran greets
   The warriors of the Fatherland.
   The religion of our Republic
   Is our shield and support.
   Freedom and welfare are the benefits
   Gained through our skill in the use of arms.
   The dark night of hardship has passed,
   The sun of our fortune has shone out.
   Under the shadow of the Qor'an
   May Iran be permanent, everlasting!

IRAQ
Land of Two Rivers

Words by
SHAFIQ ABDULJABAR AL-KAMALI (*b.* 1930)

Music by
WALID GEORGES GHOLMIEH (*b.* 1938)
Harmonised and arranged by
W.L. REED

March tempo

Adopted in 1981.
This is the abridged, vocal version. There are seven verses in all, as well as instrumental sections in the full version of this anthem.

1. *Watanun Medde Alal-ufqi Janaha*
    Warteda Majdal-hadarati Wishaha
    Burikat Ardul-furataini Watan
    Abqariyy-al-majd Azmen Wa Samaha.

2. *Hathihil-ardu Lehibun Wa Sana*
    Wa Shumukhum La Tudanini Sama
    Jabalun Yesmu Ala Hamil-duna
    Wa Suhulun Jassadat Fina-l-iba
    Babilun Fina Wa Ashourun Lena
    Wa Bina-l-tarikhu Yakhdallu Dia
    Nahnu Fin-nasi Jamana Wahduna
    Ghadbat As-sayfi Wa Hilm Al-anbiya.

3. *Ya Saraya Al-bathi Ya Usde-l-arin*
    Ya Shumukh Al-izzi Wal-majd It-talid
    Izahafi Kal-hawli Lin-nasri-l-mubin
    Wab Athi Fi Ardina Ahda-r-rashid
    Nahnu Jeel-ul-bathli Fajru-l-kadihin
    Ya Rihab Al-majd Udna Min Jadid
    Ummatun Nabni Bi Azmin La Yalim
    Wa Shahidun Yaqatfi Khatwa Shahid.

4. *Shabuna-l-jabbar Zahwun Wantilaq*
    Wa Qila Al-izzi Yebniba Al-rifag
    Dumta Lil-urbi Malathan Ya Iraq
    Wa Shumusan Tajalu-l-layla Sabaha.

Translation

1. A homeland that extended its wings over the horizon,
    And wore the glory of civilisation as a garment —
    Blessed be the land of the two rivers,
    A homeland of glorious determination and tolerance.

2. This homeland is made of flame and splendour
    And pride unequalled by the high heavens.
    It is a mountain that rises above the tops of the world
    And a plain that embodies our pride.
    Babylon is inherent in us and Assyria is ours,
    And because of the glory of our background
    History itself radiates with light,
    And it is we alone who possess the anger of the sword
    And the patience of the prophets.

3. Oh company of al-Ba'th, you pride of lions,
    Oh pinnacle of pride and of inherited glory,
    Advance, bringing terror, to a certain victory
    And resurrect the time of al-Rashid in our land!
    We are a generation who give all and toil to the utmost.

4. Oh expanse of glory, we have returned anew
    To a nation that we build with unyielding determination.
    And each martyr follows in the footsteps of a former martyr.
    Our mighty nation is filled with pride and vigour
    And the comrades build the fortresses of glory.
    Oh Iraq, may you remain for ever a refuge for all the Arabs
    And be as suns that turn night into day!

IRISH REPUBLIC
Amhrán na bhFiann
(The Soldier's Song)

Words by
PEADAR KEARNEY (1883-1942)

Music by
PATRICK HEENEY (1881-1911)
Arr. by T.M. CARTLEDGE

By permission of Minister of Finance, Éire.
Chorus adopted as National Anthem, July 1926.

tuinn   do ráin-ig   chúghainn,   Fé —— mhóid bheith saor.   Sean-
land   be-yond the   wave.   Sworn — to be   free,   No

-tír   ár sinn-sear   feas - ta Ní   fág-far fé'n tío-rán ná   fé'n
more   our an-cient sire - land Shall   shel - ter the des-pot or   the

p

tráil.   A - nocht   a thé-am   sa — bheár - na bhaoghail, Le
slave.   To - night   we man — the — bear - na baoghail* In

cresc.   *f*   *cresc.*

gean   ar Ghaedhil chun   báis nó saoghail, Le   gun - a - sgréach,   fé
Er - in's cause, come   woe or weal; 'Mid   can - nons' roar   and

cresc.   *f*   *cresc.*

* Pronounced 'Barna Bwail'. It means 'gap of danger'.

lámhach   na — bpiléar,   Seo libh,   can-aidh   Amh-rán   na bhFiann.
ri -   fles'_ peal   We'll   chant   a   sol - dier's song.

2. _Cois bánta réidhe, ar árdaibh sléibhe,_
   Ba bhuadhach ár sinnsear romhainn,
   Ag lámhach go tréan fé'n sár-bhrat séin
   Tá thuas sa ghaoith go seolta.
   Ba dhúthchas riamh d'ár gcine cháidh
   Gan iompáil siar ó imirt áir,
   'S ag siubhal mar iad i gcoinnibh námhad
   Seo libh, canaidh Amhrán na bhFiann.

   CURFÁ: Sinn-ne Fianna Fáil, etc.

3. _A bhuidhean nách fann d'fhuil Ghaoidheal is Gall,_
   Sin breacadh lae na saoirse,
   Tá sgeimhle 's sgannradh i gcroidhthibh namhad,
   Roimh ranngaibh laochra ár dtíre.
   Ár dteinte is tréith gan spréach anois,
   Sin luisne ghlé san spéir anoir,
   'S an bíodhbha i raon na bpiléar agaibh:
   Seo libh, canaidh Amhrán na bhFiann.

   CURFÁ: Sinn-ne Fianna Fáil, etc.

2. In valley green, on towering crag,
   Our fathers fought before us,
   And conquered 'neath the same old flag
   That's proudly floating o'er us.
   We're children of a fighting race,
   That never yet has known disgrace,
   And as we march, the foe to face,
   We'll chant a soldier's song.

   CHORUS: Soldiers are we, etc.

3. Sons of the Gael! Men of the Pale!
   The long watched day is breaking;
   The serried ranks of Inisfail
   Shall set the Tyrant quaking.
   Our camp fires now are burning low:
   See in the east a silv'ry glow,
   Out yonder waits the Saxon foe,
   So chant a soldier's song.

   CHORUS: Soldiers are we, etc.

ISLE OF MAN
Arrane Ashoonagh Dy Vannin

Manx National Anthem

Words by
WILLIAM HENRY GILL (1839-1923)
Manx translation by
JOHN J. KNEEN (1873-1939)

Music adapted by
WILLIAM HENRY GILL (1839-1923)
From a Traditional Manx Air

Slow and stately

mf

1. O___ Hal-loo nyn ghooie, O'___ Ch'lie-geen ny s'bwaaie
2. Lhig___ dooin bog-goil bee, Lesh___ an-nym as cree,
1. O___ land of our birth. O___ gem of God's earth,
2. Then___ let us re-joice With___ heart, soul and voice,

Ry___ ghed-dyn er ooir aa-lin Yee, Ta dt' Ard-stoyl Reill-Thie
As___ cro-ghey er gial-dyn yn Chiarn; Dy___ vod-mayd dagh oor,
O___ Is-land so strong and so fair; Built___ firm as Bar-rool,
And___ in The Lord's pro-mise con-fide; That___ each sin-gle hour

Myr___ Bar-rool er py hoie Dy___ reayll shin___ ayns___ seyr-snys as shee.___
Treish___ teil er e phooar, Dagh___ olk ass___ nyn an-mee-nyn 'hayrn.___
Thy___ Throne of Home Rule Make us free as___ thy___ sweet mountain air.___
We___ trust in His power No e-vil___ our___ souls can be-tide.___

The main National Anthem is that for Great Britain. This anthem was dedicated to The Lady Raglan, 1907. There are 8 verses in all. We give the first and last verses, which are those usually sung.

W.H. Gill, a keen Manxman, was a collector and arranger of Manx music, of which he made a special study. J.J. Kneen was an expert on the Manx language and author of several books on it. For his scholarship he was awarded the Order of St. Olaf by H.M. The King of Norway, in recognition also of the historical connection between Norway and the Isle of Man.

ISRAEL
Hatikvah
(The Hope)

Words by
NAFTALI HERZ IMBER (1856-1909)

Composer unknown

Hatikvah is now firmly established as the Anthem of the State of Israel as well as the Jewish National Anthem.

shnot al-pa-yim, Le-hiyot am chof-shi be-ar-zei-nu,__

E-rez__ zi-on viye-ru-sha-la-yim. Le hiyot am chof-shi

be-ar-zei-nu,__ E-rez zi-on viye-ru-sha-la-yim.

Free Translation

While yet within the heart - inwardly
The soul of the Jew yearns,
And towards the vistas of the East - eastwards
An eye to Zion looks.
'Tis not yet lost, our hope,
The hope of two thousand years,
To be a free people in our land
In the land of Zion and Jerusalem.

ITALY
Inno di Mameli

Words by
GOFFREDO MAMELI (1827-1849)

Music by
MICHELE NOVARO (1822-1885)

Adopted as National Anthem 2 June, 1946, on the establishment of the Republic.

Ro - ma Id - di - o la____ cre - ò.

Fratel - li d'I - ta - lia, l'I - ta - lia s'è

de - sta, dell'el - mo di Sci - pio s'è cin - ta la te - sta. Dov'è la vit-

-to - ria? Le por - ga la chio - ma, che schia - va di Ro - ma Iddio la cre-

Free Translation

Italian Brothers,
Italy has arisen,
Has put on the helmet of Scipio.
Where is Victory?
Created by God
The slave of Rome,
She crowns you with glory.
Let us unite,
We are ready to die,
Italy calls.

IVORY COAST
L'Abidjanaise

Words by
MATHIEU EKRA (*b.* 1917)
in collaboration with **JOACHIM BONY**
and the Abbé **COTY**

Music by
PIERRE MICHEL PANGO (*b.* 1926) and
PIERRE MARIE COTY (*b.* 1927)
Arr. by **HENRY COLEMAN**

Salut ô ter-re d'es-pé-ran-ce;
Pa-ys de l'hos-pi-ta-li-té. Tes lé-gions rem-plies de vail-lan-ce Ont re-le-vé ta di-gni-té.

Tes fils chè-re Côte d'I-voi-re
Fiers ar-ti-sans de ta gran-deur, Tous ras-sem-blés et pour ta gloi-re Te bâ-ti-ront dans le bon-

This National Anthem was adopted at the declaration of independence on 7 August, 1960.
Mathieu Ekra was Minister of Information and Joachim Bony was Minister of Education in the Ivory Coast.

à l'hu - ma - ni - té, En for-geant, u - nie dans la

foi nou - vel - le, la pa-trie de la vraie fra - ter - ni - té.

Paraphrase by
Elizabeth P. Coleman

We salute you, O land of hope, country of hospitality;
thy gallant legions have restored thy dignity.

Beloved Ivory Coast, thy sons, proud builders of thy
greatness, all mustered together for thy glory,
in joy will construct thee.

Proud citizens of the Ivory Coast, the country calls us.
If we have brought back liberty peacefully, it will be
our duty to be an example of the hope promised to humanity,
forging unitedly in new faith the Fatherland of true
brotherhood.

JAMAICA

Words by
HUGH SHERLOCK (*b.* 1905)

Music by
ROBERT LIGHTBOURNE (*b.* 1909)
Arr. by MAPLETOFT POULLE

This was officially selected as the National Anthem by the House of Representatives on 19 July, 1962. Robert Lightbourne was Minister of Trade and Industry at the time of composing the Anthem.

JAPAN

Words selected from the seventh volume
of *Kokinshu* dating from the 9th century
English translation by
SAKUZO TAKADA

Music by
HIROMORI HAYASHI (1831-1896)

Ki - mi - ga___ yo___ wa Chi - yo - ni___
May thy peace-ful reign last long! May it last for

Ya - chi - yo - ni Sa - za - ré - i - shi no, I - wa - o to
thou-sands of years, Un - til this ti - ny stone will grow in - to a

na - ri - té, Ko - ké no mu - su___ ma - dé.
mas - sive rock And the moss will cov - er it all deep and thick.

First performed on 3 November, 1880, on the Emperor Meiji's birthday, and approved as National Anthem on
12 August, 1893.

JORDAN

Words by
ABDUL-MONE'M AL-RIFAI' (*b.* 1917)

Music by
ABDUL-QADER AL-TANEER (1901-1957)

Free Translation

Long live the King!
Long live the King!
His position is sublime,
His banners waving in glory supreme.

Adopted as National Anthem when Emir Abdullah became King, 25 May, 1946.

KAMPUCHEA

Transliteration and translation by
JUDITH M. JACOB

Arranged and harmonised by
W.L. REED

March tempo

Jhām kra-ham crāl scor srab kruṅ vāl kam-bu-jā mā-tu-bhūm(i) jham kam-ma-kar Ka-se-kar ṭa ut-tam jhām yud-dha-jan yud-dha-na-ri pa-ṭi-

Adopted in 1976.

Translation

The bright red blood was spilled over the towns
and over the plain of Kampuchea, our motherland,
the blood of our good workers and farmers and of
our revolutionary combatants, both men and women.

Their blood produced a great anger and the courage
to contend with heroism. On the 17th. of April,
under the revolutionary banner, their blood freed
us from the state of slavery.

Hurrah for the 17th. of April!
That wonderful victory had greater significance
than the Angkor period!

We are uniting to construct a Kampuchea with a
new and better society, democratic, egalitarian
and just. We follow the road to a firmly-based
independence. We absolutely guarantee to defend
our motherland. our fine territory, our
magnificent revolution!

Hurrah for the new Kampuchea, a splendid,
democratic land of plenty! We guarantee to raise
aloft and wave the red banner of the revolution.
We shall make our motherland properous beyond
all others, magnificent, wonderful!

KENYA

Words written collectively

Composer unknown

The first line of each verse, * to *, may be sung by a soloist in the African traditional style.

The National Anthem is based on a traditional Kenya Folk Song which was adapted and harmonised by a National Commission of Musicians who also wrote the words.

2. Let one and all arise
   With hearts both strong and true.
   Service be our earnest endeavour,
   And our Homeland of Kenya,
   Heritage of splendour,
   Firm may we stand to defend.

3. Let all with one accord
   In common bond united,
   Build this our nation together,
   And the glory of Kenya,
   The fruit of our labour
   Fill every heart with thanksgiving.

KIRIBATI

Words and music by
IOTEBA TAMUERA URIAM (*b.* 1910)

Andante (♩=102)

1. Tei - ra - ke kai-ni Ki - ri - ba - ti, A - ne-ne ma te kā - ka-to - nga,

Tau - ra - oi na-kon te nwi - o - ko, Ma ni bu-o-ki - a ao - ma - ta.

Ta - ua - ni - nne n te ___ ra - oi - roi, Ta-ngi-ri - a ao - ma ta na - ko.

Ta - ua - ni nne n te ___ ra - oi - roi, Ta-ngi-ri - a ao - ma - ta.

Independence was achieved on 12 July, 1979, when this anthem was first sung.

2. *Reken te kabaia ma te rau*
   Ibuakoia kaain abara
   Bon reken te nano ae banin
   Ma te i-tangitangiri naba.
   Ma ni wakina te kab'aia,
   Ma n neboa i eta abara.
   Ma ni wakina te kab'aia,
   Ma n neboa abara.

3. *Ti butiko ngkoe Atuara*
   Kawakinira ao kairira
   Nakon taai aika i maira.
   Buokira ni baim ae akoi.
   Kakabaia ara Tautaeka
   Ma ake a makuri iai.
   Kakabaia ara Tautaeka
   Ma aomata ni bane.

Translation

1. Stand up, Gilbertese!
   Sing with jubilation!
   Prepare to accept responsibility
   And to help each other!
   Be steadfastly righteous!
   Love all our people!
   Be steadfastly righteous!
   Love all our people!

2. The attainment of contentment
   And peace by our people
   Will be achieved when all
   Our hearts beat as one,
   Love one another!
   Promote happiness and unity!
   Love one another!
   Promote happiness and unity!

3. We beseech You, O God,
   To protect and lead us
   In the days to come.
   Help us with Your loving hand.
   Bless our Government
   And all our people!
   Bless our Government
   And all our people!

KOREA (North)
Democratic Republic of Korea

Words by
PAK SE YONG (*b.* 1902)

Music by
KIM WON GYUN (*b.* 1912)

261

Fairly slowly and solemnly

1. A ch'im ŭn pin - na - ra, i kang-san ŭn - gum e, cha - wŏn do ka - dŭk han sam - ch'ŏl - li, a - rŭm-da-un nae cho-guk, pan - man-nyŏn ora-en ryŏk-sa e ch'al - lan han mun-hwa ro cha - ra-nan sŭl - gi - roun in - min ŭi i yŏng-gwang: Mom_

Adopted in 1947 but no further information available.

gwa mam ta__ pa-ch'yǒ, i, cho-sǒn kir - i____ pat - tǔ - se. Ch'al- se.

2. *Paektusan kisang ǔl ta anko.*
    Kǔllo ǔi chǒngsin ǔn kittǔrǒ.
    Chilli ro mungch 'yǒ jin ǒksen ttǔt
    On segye apsǒ nagari.
    Sonnǔn him nodo do naemirǒ,
    Inmin ǔi ttǔs ǔro sǒn nara.
    Han ǒpsi pugang hanǔn
    I chosǒn kiri pinnaese.

Translation

1. Let morning shine on the silver and gold of this land,
    Three thousand leagues packed with natural wealth.
    My beautiful fatherland.
    The glory of a wise people
    Brought up in a culture brilliant
    With a history five millenia long.
    Let us devote our bodies and minds
    To supporting this Korea for ever.

2. The firm will, bonded with truth,
    Nest for the spirit of labour,
    Embracing the atmosphere of Mount Paektu,
    Will go forth to all the world.
    The country established by the will of the people,
    Breasting the raging waves with soaring strength.
    Let us glorify for ever this Korea,
    Limitlessly rich and strong.

KOREA (South)
Republic of Korea

Author unknown
English versification by
WHAMI KOH and
T.M. CARTLEDGE

Music by
EAK TAY AHN (1906-1965)

1. Tong - hai Mool - kwa Paik - tu - san - i Ma - ru - go Tal - to -
2. Nam - san U - ye Chu - so - na - mu Chul - kap - eul Tur - ul -
1. Tong - Hai Sea and Pak - doo Moun - tain, So long as they en -
2. E - ter - nal - ly Naam - saan's pine - trees Stand like an ar - mour

- rok Ha - na - nim - i Po - ho - ha - sa
- tut Pa - ram - i - sul Pul - byun - ha - mum
- dure, May God bless Ko - re - a our land For
sure, Through what - ev - er tem - pest or dan - ger,

Talt - to - rok
Tur - ul - tut
en - dure, ___
like ar - mour,

This song, of unknown authorship, was set originally to a different tune and sung in Korea for many years. When the Government of the Republic of Korea was established on 15 August, 1948, these verses, with the music by Eak Tay Ahn, were officially adopted as the National Anthem.

CHORUS

U - ri na - ra Man - sei.
U - ri ki - sang Il - sae.
end - less a - ges to come!
As our sym - bol of strength.

Moo - gung - wha
North to South be -

Man - sei.____
Il - sae.____
end - less a - ges!
as our sym - bol.

Sam - chul - ri Hwa - ryu Kang - san,____
- decked with flow - ers, Land of beau - ty rare,____

Hwa - ryu Kang - san, Hwa - ryu - han.
land of beau - ty, land of beau - ty.

Tae - han Sa - ram Tae - han____ eu - ro Ki - ri Po - chun - ha - sae.
May God keep our coun - try u - nit - ed And pre - serve our land.

KUWAIT

No words*

Music by
IBRAHIM NASIR AL-SOULA (*b.* 1935)
Transcribed and arranged by
W.L. REED

The above is the new National Anthem, used for ceremonial occasions, without words. *There is a longer version, with words by **AHMAD MUSHARI AL-ADWANI** (*b.* 1923), which is used as the National Song.
Adopted in 1978.

LAOS

Words by
SISANA SISANE (*b.* 1922)

Music by
THONGDY SOUNTHONEVICHIT (*b.* 1905)

Xat - lao tang-tae day - ma lao thook -thua - na xeut-xoo soo -tchay, Huam-

haeng huam-chit huam - chay sa - mak-khi - kan pen kam-lang di - ao. Det -

diao phom-kan kao - na boo - xa xü - kiat khong lao, Song -

Adopted in 1947. New text adopted in 1975.

Translation

For all time the Lao people have glorified their Fatherland,
United in heart, spirit and vigour as one.
Resolutely moving forwards, respecting and increasing the dignity of the Lao people
And proclaiming the right to be their own masters.
The Lao people of all origins are equal and will no longer allow imperialists and traitors to harm them.
The entire people will safeguard the independence and the freedom of the Lao nation.
They are resolved to struggle for victory in order to lead the nation to prosperity.

LEBANON

Words by
RACHID NAKHLÉ (1873-1939)

Music by
WADIH SABRA (1876-1952)

1. *Koul - lou - na*   *Lil - oua - tann Lil -'ou - la   Lil 'a*
2. *Chay-khou - na*   *Oual - fa - ta   In - da-saôu - til   Oua*
3. *Bah - rou - hou*   *Bar - rou - hou Dour - ra - touch - char*

Adopted officially by Presidential decree on 12 July, 1927.

Lam,   Mil - ou 'ay   Niz - za - man   Say - fou - na   Oual Ka-
Tann   Ous - dou ghâ   Bin Ma - ta   Sa - oua - rat   Nal - fi-
Kain   Ril - dou - hou   Bir - rou - hou   Ma - li - oul   Kout-

-lam,   Sah - lou - na   Oual - ja - bal   Man - bi
-tann   Char - kou - na   Kal - bou - hou   A - ba
-baïn   Is - mou - hou   'Iz - zou - hou   Moun Zou

Tonn   Lir - ri - jâl,   Kaou - lou - na   Oual 'A - mal   Fi - sa
Dann   Loub - nane   Sa - na - hou   Rab Bou - hou   Li - ma-
Kâ - nal   Jou - doude   Maj - dou - hu   Ar - zou - hou   Ram - zou-

Free Translation

1. All of us! For our Country, for our Flag and Glory!
Our valour and our writings are the envy of the ages.
Our mountains and our valleys, they bring forth stalwart men.
And to Perfection all our efforts we devote.
All of us! For our Country, for our Flag and Glory!

2. Our Elders and our children, they await our Country's call:
And on the Day of Crisis they are as Lions of the Jungle.
The heart of our East is ever Lebanon:
May God preserve her until end of time.
All of us! For our Country, for our Flag and Glory!

3. The Gems of the East are her land and sea.
Throughout the world her good deeds flow from pole to pole.
And her name is her glory since time began.
Immortality's Symbol— the Cedar— is her Pride.
All of us! For our Country, for our Flag and Glory!

LESOTHO

Words by
FRANÇOIS COILLARD (1834-1904)

Music by
FERDINAND-SAMUEL LAUR (1791-1854)

1. *Le-so-tho fa-tŝe la bo-nta-t'a ro-na, Ha-r'a ma-fa-tŝe le le-tle ke lo-na. Ke moo re hla-hi-leng, Ke moo re ho-li-leng, Re-a le ra-ta.*

2. *Molimo ak'u boloke Lesotho,*
   U felise lintoa le matŝoenyeho.
   Oho fatŝe lena,
   La bo-ntat'a rona,
   Le be le khotso.

Translation

1. Lesotho, land of our Fathers,
   You are the most beautiful country of all.
   You give us birth,
   In you we are reared
   And you are dear to us.

2. Lord, we ask You to protect Lesotho.
   Keep us free from conflict and tribulations.
   Oh, land of mine,
   Land of our Fathers,
   May you have peace.

The Government adopted this as their National Anthem on 2 May, 1967, using the first and last verses of the words written by a French missionary.

LIBERIA

Words by
DANIEL BASHIEL WARNER *(1815-1880)

Music by
OLMSTEAD LUCA (b. 1836)†

Moderato

1. All hail, Li - be - ria, hail! All hail, Li - be - ria,
2. All hail, Li - be - ria, hail! All hail, Li - be - ria,

hail! This glo - rious land of li - ber - ty Shall
hail! In u - nion strong suc - cess is sure— We

long be ours.___ Though new her name, Green be her fame, And
can - not fail!___ With God a - bove Our rights to prove We

*Third President of Liberia, 1864-1868.
†Year of death unknown.

migh - ty be her powers,_____
will o'er all pre - vail,_____

And migh - ty be her powers._____
We will o'er all pre - vail!_____

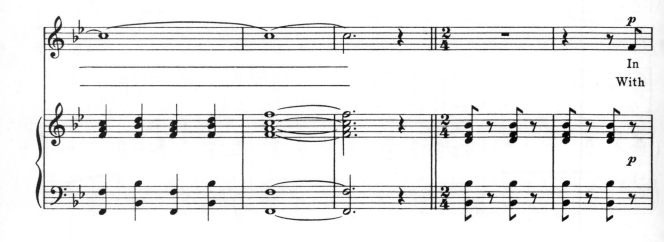

In
With

LIBYAN ARAB JAMAHIRIYA

Words by
A. SHAMSEDDEIN *

Music by
M. CHAREIF

Libya became a republic in September 1969.
* It has not been possible to obtain the words.

LIECHTENSTEIN

Words by
JAKOB JOSEF JAUCH *(d. 1859)

Composer unknown †

Moderato

1. O - ben am deut - schen Rhein leh - net sich Liech - ten-stein
2. Wo einst Sankt Lu - zi - en Frie - den nach Rä - ti - en

an Al - pen - höh'n. Dies lie - be Hei - mat-land im deut-schen
hin - ein ge - bracht, dort an dem Gren - zen-stein und längs dem

Va - ter-land hat Got - tes__ wei - se Hand für uns er - seh'n.
jun - gen Rhein steht furcht-los__ Liech - ten-stein auf Deutschlands Wacht.

The words were written in 1850.
The tune is the same as that of the National Anthem of Great Britain.
*Year of birth unknown.
†See Great Britain.

3. *Lieblich zur Sommerzeit*
    Auf hoher Alpenweid
    Schwebt Himmelsruh,
    Wo frei die Gemse springt,
    Kühn sich der Adler schwingt,
    Der Senn' das Ave singt
    Der Heimat zu.

4. *Von grüngen Felsenhöhn*
    Freundlich ist es zu sehn
    Mit einem Blick,
    Wie des Rheines Silberband
    Säumet das schöne Land,
    Ein kleines Vaterland
    Voll stillen Glücks.

5. *Hoch lebe Liechtenstein,*
    Blühend am deutschen Rhein,
    Glücklich und treu.
    Hoch leb der Fürst vom Land,
    Hoch unser Vaterland,
    Durch Bruderliebe Band
    Vereint und frei.

Free Translation

1. High above the German Rhine
    Leans Liechtenstein
    Against Alpine slopes.
    This beloved homeland
    In the German fatherland
    Was chosen for us by
    The Lord's wisdom.

2. Where once St. Lucius
    Brought peace to Rätien,
    There on the boundary-stone
    And along the young Rhine
    Stands dauntless Liechtenstein
    On Germany's guard.

3. Lovely in summer-time
    On high Alpine pastures
    Floats heavenly peace,
    Where the chamois freely jumps about,
    The eagle sways boldly in the air,
    The herdsman sings the 'Ave'
    Towards the homeland.

4. From high green rocks
    It is a lovely sight to watch
    How the silvery ribbon of the Rhine
    Edges the beautiful country,
    A small fatherland,
    Full of quiet happiness.

5. Long live Liechtenstein,
    Blossoming on the German Rhine,
    Happy and faithful.
    Long live the Duke of the Land,
    Long live our fatherland,
    United by brotherly bonds and free.

LUXEMBOURG
Ons Hémécht
(Our Motherland)

Words by
MICHEL LENTZ (1820-1893)
Translation by
NICHOLAS E. WEYDERT

Music by
JEAN-ANTOINE ZINNEN (1827-1898)
Arr. by MARTIN SHAW

1. Wŏ d'Uol - zécht du - réch d'Wi - sen zĕt durch d'Fiel - zen d'Sau - er
1. Where slow you see the Al - zet - te flow, The Su - ra__ play wild

brécht, Wŏ d'Riéf lauscht d'Mu - sel dof - tég blet, den Him - mel Wein ons
pranks, Where love - ly vine - yards am - ply grow Up - on the Mo - selle's

mécht;___ Dât ass ons Land fir dât mer gĕf hei -
banks,___ There lies the land for which our thanks Are

First performed 5 June, 1864, this became the National Anthem in 1895. There are four verses in all.
Words copyright J.B. Cramer & Co. Ltd.

2. *O Du do uewen, dém seng Hand*
   Durch d'Welt d'Natio'ne lêd,
   Behitt Du d'Letzeburger Land
   Vum friéme Joch a Lêd.
   Du hues ons all als Kanner schon
   De freie Gêscht jo gin;
   Lôss viru blénken d'Freihêtssonn,
   De' mir 'so' lâng gesin.
   Lôss viru blénken d'Freihêtssonn,
   De' mir 'so' lâng gesin.

2. Oh Father in Heaven,Whose powerful hand
   Makes states or lays them low,
   Protect the Luxembourger land
   From foreign yoke and woe.
   God's golden liberty bestow
   On us now as of yore.
   Let Freedom's sun in glory glow
   For now and evermore.

MALAGASY

Words by
Pasteur RAHAJASON (1897-1971)

Music by
NORBERT RAHARISOA *(d. 1964)
Arr. by HENRY COLEMAN

Adopted on 21 October, 1958 by Madagascar.
The name of the country was changed to Malagasy on 26 June, 1960.

* Year of birth unknown.

CHORUS

-hi - onao ry Za-na-ha - ry 'Ty No-si-ndrazanay i-

-ty____ Hi - a - da-na sy ho fi - na - ri-tra He

sa-mba-tra to-koa i - za-hay____ Ta hay.

Translation

1. O, our beloved fatherland,
   O, fair Madagascar,
   Our love will never decay,
   But will last eternally.

2. O, our beloved fatherland,
   Let us be thy servant
   With body, heart and spirit
   In dear and worthy service.

3. O, our beloved fatherland,
   May God bless thee,
   That created all lands;
   In order He maintains thee.

CHORUS O, Lord Creator, do Thou bless
This Island of our Fathers,
That she may be happy and prosperous
For our own satisfaction.

MALAWI

Words* and music by
MICHAEL-FREDRICK PAUL SAUKA (*b.* 1934)

1. O God bless our land of Ma - la - wi,
1. *Mlu - ngu da - li - tsa - ni Ma - la - wi,*

Keep it a land of peace.
Mum - su - nge m'mte - nde - re.
Put down each and
Go - nje - tsa - ni

ev - ery e - ne - my,
a - da - ni o - nse,
Hung - er, dis - ease, en - vy.
Nja - la, nthe - nda, nsa - nje.

* The official text is given in English and Chichewa. The Chitumbuka version is no longer used.

Copyright, 1964, Government of Malawi.
This National Anthem was selected as a result of a competition held in February 1964.
It was first played publicly on Independence Day, 6 July, 1964.

English

2. Our own Malawi, this land so fair,
   Fertile and brave and free.
   With its lakes, refreshing mountain air,
   How greatly blest are we.
   Hills and valleys, soil so rich and rare,
   Give us a bounty free.
   Wood and forest, plains so broad and fair,
   All-beauteous Malawi.

3. Freedom ever, let us all unite
   To build up Malawi.
   With our love, our zeal and loyalty,
   Bringing our best to her.
   In time of war, or in time of peace,
   One purpose and one goal.
   Men and women serving selflessly
   In building Malawi.

Chichewa

2. *Malawi ndziko lokongola,*
   La chonde ndi ufulu,
   Nyanja ndi mphepo ya m'mapiri,
   Ndithudi tadala.
   Zigwa, mapiri, nthaka, dzinthu,
   N'mphatso zaulere.
   Nkhalango, madambo abwino.
   Ngwokoma Malawi.

3. *O! Ufulu tigwirizane,*
   Kukweza Malawi.
   Ndi chikondi, khama, kumvera,
   Timutumikire.
   Pa nkhondo nkana pa mtendere,
   Cholinga n'chimodzi.
   Mai, bambo, tidzipereke,
   Pokweza Malawi.

MALAYASIA

Words written collectively

Music by
PIERRE JEAN de BERANGER (1780-1857)

Ne - ga - ra ku Ta - nah tum - pah - nya da - rah ku,_____ Rak - yat hi - dup ber - sa - tu dan ma - ju,_____ Rah - mat bah - gia tu -

Adopted as National Anthem when Malaya achieved independence on 31 August, 1957. It was previously known in Malaya and Indonesia as a popular song called Terang Bulan (Moonlight), but this popular version of the tune is now banned. When Malaysia was founded in 1963 this was retained as the National Anthem.

Free Translation

My country,
The land of my birth.
May her people live in unity and prosperity,
May God grant His blessings upon her.
Peacefully may our Ruler reign.
May God grant His blessings upon her.
Peacefully may our Ruler reign.

MALDIVES

Words by
MOHAMED JAMEEL DIDI (*b.* 1915)

Music by
WANNAKUWATTAWADUGE DON AMARADEVA
(*b.* 1927)
Arranged from band score by
W. L. REED

This melody replaced the former one on 13 March, 1972.

D.C. al Fine

Gavmii mi ekuverikan matii tibegen kuriime salaam,
Gavmii bahun gina heyo du'aa kuramun kuriime salaam.
Gavmii nishaanang hurmataa eku boo lambai tibegen
Audaanakan libigen e vaa dida-ak kuriime salaam.
Nasraa nasiibaa kaamyaabu-ge ramzakang himenee
Fessaa rataai hudaa ekii fenumun kuriime salaam.
Fakhraa sharaf gavmang e hoodai devvi batalunna'
Zikraage mativeri ḥentakun adugai kuriime salaam.
Divehiinge ummay kuri arai silmaa salaamatugai
Divehiinge nan moḷu vun adai tibegen kuriime salaam.
Minivankamaa madaniyyataa libigen mi 'aalamugai
Dinigen hitaamatakun tibun edigen kuriime salaam.
Diinaai verinnang heyo hitun hurmay adaa kuramun
Siidaa vafaaterikan matii tibegen kuriime salaam.
Davlatuge aburaa 'izzataa mativeri vegen abada'
Audaana vun edi heyo du'aa kuramun kuriime salaam.

Translation

We salute you in this national unity.
We salute you, with many good wishes in the national tongue,
Bowing the head in respect to the national symbol.
We salute the flag that has such might;
It falls into the sphere of victory, fortune and success
With its green and red and white together, and therefore we salute it.
To those heroes who sought out honour and pride for the nation
We give salute today in auspicious verses of remembrance.
May the nation of the Maldivian Islanders advance under guard and protection
And the name of the Maldivian Islanders become great. Thus we pledge as we salute.
We wish for their freedom and progress in this world
And for their freedom from sorrows, and thus we salute.
With full respect and heartfelt blessing towards religion and our leaders,
We salute you in uprightness and truth.
May the State ever have auspicious honour and respect.
With good wishes for your continuing might, we salute you.

MALI

Words by
M'PÉ BENGALY (*b.* 1928)
and others

Music by
BANZOUMANA SISSOKO (*b.* circa 1890)
Arr. by HENRY COLEMAN

Lyrics under the music:

1. A ton ap-pel, MA-LI, Pour ta pros-pé-ri-té Fi-dèle à ton des-tin Nous se-rons tous u-nis, Un peuple, un but, u-ne foi. _____ Pour une A-frique u-nie Si l'en-ne-mi découvre son front Au de-dans ou au de-hors De-bout sur les rem-

This National Anthem was adopted by the National Assembly on 9 August, 1962.

-parts Nous som-mes ré - so - lus de mou - rir.

Chorus

Pour l'A - frique et pour toi MA - LI
-LI au - jour-d'hui O MA-LI de de - main Les champs fleu-

rall. 2nd time

No - tre dra-peau se - ra li - ber - té.
-ris - sent d'es - pé - ran - ce, Les coeurs vi - brent de con -

rall. 2nd time

1.

Pour l'A-frique et pour toi MA - LI

No - tre com - bat se - ra u - ni - té.   O MA- fian - ce.

2. *Debout, villes et campagnes,*
   Debout, femmes, jeunes et vieux
   Pour la Patrie en marche
   Vers l'avenir radieux
   Pour notre dignité.
   Renforçons bien nos rangs,
   Pour le salut public
   Forgeons le bien commun
   Ensemble, au coude à coude
   Faisons le chantier du bonheur.

   Chorus   *Pour l'Afrique et pour toi, MALI etc.*

3. *La voie est dure, très dure*
   Qui mène au bonheur commun.
   Courage et dévouement,   } (bis.)
   Vigilance à tout moment,
   Vérité des temps anciens,
   Vérité de tous les jours,
   Le bonheur par le labeur
   Fera le MALI de demain.

   Chorus   *Pour l'Afrique et pour toi, MALI etc.*

4. *L'Afrique se lève enfin*
   Saluons ce jour nouveau.
   Saluons la liberté,
   Marchons vers l'unité.
   Dignité retrouvée
   Soutient notre combat.
   Fidèles à notre serment
   De faire l'Afrique unie
   Ensemble, debout mes frères
   Tous au rendez-vous de l'honneur.

   Chorus   *Pour l'Afrique et pour toi, MALI etc.*

Translation by
T.M. Cartledge

1. At your call, MALI,
So that you may prosper,
Faithful to your destiny,
We shall all be united,
One people, one goal, one faith
For a united Africa.
If the enemy should show himself
Within or without,
On the ramparts
We are ready to stand and die.

Chorus   For Africa and for you, MALI,
Our banner shall be liberty.
For Africa and for you, MALI,
Our fight shall be for unity.
Oh, MALI of today,
Oh, MALI of tomorrow,
The fields are flowering with hope
And hearts are thrilling with confidence.

2. Stand up, towns and countryside,
Stand up, women, stand up young and old,
For the Fatherland on the road
Towards a radiant future.
For the sake of our dignity
Let us strengthen our ranks;
For the public well-being
Let us forge the common good.
Together, shoulder to shoulder,
Let us work for happiness.

3. The road is hard, very hard,
That leads to common happiness.
Courage and devotion,
Constant vigilance,
Courage and devotion,
Constant vigilance,
Truth from olden times,
The truths of every day,
Happiness through effort
Will build the MALI of tomorrow.

4. Africa is at last arising,
Let us greet this new day.
Let us greet freedom,
Let us march towards unity.
Refound dignity
Supports our struggle.
Faithful to our oath
To make a united Africa,
Together, arise, my brothers,
All to the place where honour calls.

MALTA

Words by
DUN KARM PSAILA (1871-1961)
Translation by
MAY BUTCHER

Music by
ROBERT SAMMUT (1870-1934)

Dun Karm Psaila, Malta's greatest poet, was asked to write these words for a school hymn to Sammut's music. He conceived the idea of writing a hymn to Malta in the form of a prayer; he wanted to unite all parties with the strong ties of religion and love of country.

It was first performed on 3 February, 1923, and later declared to be the official anthem on 7 April, 1941.

land_____ so dear whose name___ we___ bear!_____
- lej,_____ Kif dej - jem Int___ ha - rist:_____
mer - cy, strength in man___ in - crease!_____
- na_____ lis - sid, sah - ha___ 'l - had - di - em.

Keep her in mind____ whom Thou hast made so___ fair!_____
Fta - kar li lil - ha bil - oh - la dawl lib - bist!_____
Con - firm us all_____ in u - ni - ty___ and_ peace!_____
Sed - daq il - ghaq - da fil - Mal - tin u___ s - sliem!_____

MAURITANIA

No words

Music by
TOLIA NIKIPROWETZKY (*b.* 1916)

Based on traditional music, this was adopted as the National Anthem in 1960, the year of Independence.

298

come sopra

simile

eome sopra

simile

D. 𝄋 al Fine

MAURITIUS

Words by
JEAN GEORGES PROSPER (*b.* 1933)

Music by
PHILIPPE GENTIL (*b.* 1928)

This National Anthem, which was selected by means of a competition, came into use when the country attained independence on 12 March, 1968.

one peo-ple, As one na-tion, For peace, jus-tice and li-ber-

ty. Be - lov - - ed coun-try, may

God bless thee For e - ver and e - - ver.

MEXICO

Words by
FRANCISCO GONZÁLEZ BOCANEGRA (1824-1861)
Translation by
B. ROMERO
Versified by
J.E. HALES

Music by
JAIME NUNÓ (1824-1908)

Poem first performed 16 September, 1854, at the National Theatre, to a different setting. Later the poem, set to Nunó's music, was selected through a government competition.

da - do en ca - da hi - jo te dió.
ev - 'ry___ one shall be found.

2. *¡Patria! ¡Patria! Tus hijos te juran*
   Exhalar en tus aras su aliento,
   Si el clarín, con su bélico acento,
   Los convoca a lidiar con valor.
   ¡Para ti las guirnaldas de oliva!
   ¡Un recuerdo para ellos de gloria!
   ¡Un laurel para ti de victoria!
   ¡Un sepulcro para ellos de honor!

   CORO: *Mexicanos, etc.*

2. Blessed Homeland, thy children have vowed them
   If the bugle to battle should call,
   They will fight with the last breath allowed them
   Till on thy loved altars they fall.
   Let the garland of olive thine be;
   Unto them be deathless fame;
   Let the laurel of victory be assigned thee,
   Enough for them the tomb's honoured name.

   CHORUS: Mexicans, etc.

MONACO

Words by
THÉOPHILE BELLANDO (1820-1903)

Composer unknown
Arr. by HENRY COLEMAN

1. Prin-ci-pau-té Mo-na-co ma pa-tri-e, Oh! com-bien Dieu est pro-di-gue pour toi. Ciel tou-jours pur, ri-ves tou-jours fleu-ri-es, Ton Sou-ve-rain est plus ai-mé qu'un

Performed for the first time in 1867 as a National Anthem. The music is based on a folk song used to Bellando's words as a marching song by the Guarde Nationale, in which Bellando served as a captain.

Roi. Ton Sou - ve-rain est plus ai-mé qu'un Roi.

2. *Fiers Compagnons de la Garde Civique,*
   Respectons tous la voix du Commandant.
   Suivons toujours notre bannière antique.
   Le tambour bat, marchons tous en Avant. (bis)

3. *Oui, Monaco connut toujours des braves.*
   Nous sommes tous leurs dignes descendants.
   En aucun temps nous ne fûmes esclaves,
   Et loin de nous, régnèrent les tyrans. (bis)

4. *Que le nom d'un Prince plein de clémence*
   Soit repété par mille et mille chants.
   Nous mourons tous pour sa propre défense,
   Mais après nous, combattrons nos enfants. (bis)

Translation

1. Principality of Monaco, my country,
   Oh! how God is lavish with you.
   An ever-clear sky, ever-blossoming shores,
   Your Sovereign is better liked than a King. (repeat)

2. Proud Fellows of the Civic Guard,
   Let us all listen to the Commander's voice.
   Let us always follow our ancient flag.
   Drums are beating, let us all march forward. (repeat)

3. Yes, Monaco always had brave men.
   We all are their worthy descendants.
   We never were slaves,
   And far from us ruled the tyrants. (repeat)

4. Let the name of a Prince full of clemency
   Be repeated in thousands and thousands of songs.
   We shall all die in his defence,
   But after us, our children will fight. (repeat)

MONGOLIA

Words by
TSEVEGMIDDIIN GAITAV (1929-1979)
and **CHOIJILYN CHIMID** (*b.* 1927)

Music by
BILEGIIN DAMDINSÜREN (*b.* 1919)

The music was adopted in 1950, and the words in 1961.

Bugd nai - ram - dakh ul - saa____ bai - guul - san.

CHORUS

Sai - khan Mon - go - lyn tsel - ger o - ron. Sa - ru - ul kheg - zhli - in

del - ger gu - ren. U - ei - in u - ed

enkh - zhin ba - dar - tu - gai. U - riin urd bekh - zhin mand - tu - gai.____

2. *Achit nam ulsyg giiguulzh,*
   Khuchit tumen ulsyg khegzhuulzh,
   Butsashgui zulgeleer duuren khevchilsen,
   Tsutsashgui temtsleer tuukhiig tovchilson.

Chorus. *Saikhan Mongolyn etc.*

3. *Zevlelt orontoi zayaa kholbozh,*
   Devshilt olontoi sanaa niilzh,
   Khandakh zugiig bakhtai bar'san,
   Mandakh Kommunizmig tsogtoi zorson.

Chorus. *Saikhan Mongolyn etc.*

Translation

1. By doing away with the former hardship and suffering,
   By setting up the rights and the happiness of the people,
   By setting up the People's Republic
   Voicing the determination of all,

Chorus. The beautiful and magnificent land of Mongolia,
   The widespread and bountiful nation
   Shall increase strongly generation after generation.
   May she rise strong from offspring to offspring!

2. The caring Party enlightens the nation,
   The stalwart multitudes develop the land;
   Dauntless efforts are in full sway,
   The tireless struggle makes history.

Chorus. (As above)

3. By linking her destiny with the Soviet Union,
   By joining her heart with the progressive nations,
   By following steadfastly the right path,
   The course towards Communism is clear.

Chorus. (As above)

MOROCCO
Hymne Cherifien

Words by
ALI SQUALLI HOUSSAINI (*b.* 1932)

Composer unknown

Manbit Al-ahrar   Masriq Al-anwar
Muntada Al-su'dad Wa-hamah
Dumt Muntadah Wa-hamah
Isht Fil-awtan   Lil-ala Unwan
Mil' Kull Janaan   Thikr Kull Lisan
Bil-rooh   Bil-jasad
Habba Fataak   Labbaa Nidaak
Fi Fammee   Wa Fi Dammee
Hawaak Thar   Noor Wa Naar
Ikhwatee Hayyaa   Lil-ala Saayeea
Nushhid Ad-dunya   Anna Huna
Nuhayya Bi-sha'aar
Allah   Al-Watan   Al-Malek

Translation

Fountain of Freedom   Source of Light
Where sovereignty and safety meet,
Safety and sovereignty   May you ever combine!
You have lived among nations   With title sublime,
Filling each heart,   Sung by each tongue,
Your champion has risen   And answered your call.
In my mouth   And in my blood
Your breezes have stirred   Both light and fire.
Up! my brethren,   Strive for the highest.
We call to the world   That we are here ready.
We salute as our emblem
God, Homeland and King.

MOZAMBIQUE

Words and music by
JUSTINO SIGAULANE CHEMANE (*b.* 1923)
Arr. by W.L. REED

Adopted in 1975, when the country became independent.

pun - ho O co - lo - nia - lis - mo der - ru - bou._____ To - do o Po - vo u-

ni - do Des - de o Ro - vu - ma a - téo Ma - pu - to,

Lu - ta contr - a im - pe - ria - lis - mo Con - ti - nua e sem - pre ven - ce -

CHORUS

ra._____ Vi - va Mo - çam - bi - que!

Vi - va a Ban-dei - ra, sím - bo - lo Na - cio-nal! Vi - va Mo - çam-

bi - que! Que por ti o Po - vo lu - ta - rá. rá.

2. *Unido ao mundo inteiro,*
Lutando contra a burguesia,
Nossa Pátria será túmulo
Do capitalismo e exploração.
O Povo Moçambicano
D'operários e de camponeses,
Engajado no trabalho
A riqueza sempre brotará.

Translation

1. **Long live FRELIMO**
Guide of the Mozambican people,
Heroic people who, gun in hand,
    toppled colonialism.
All the People united
From the Rovuma to the Maputo,
Struggle against imperialism
And continue, and shall win.

2. United with the whole world,
Struggling against the bourgeoisie,
Our country will be the tomb
Of capitalism and exploitation.
The Mozambican People,
Workers and peasants,
Engaged in work
Shall always produce wealth.

Chorus   Long live Mozambique!
Long live our flag, symbol of the Nation!
Long live Mozambique!
For thee your People will fight.

NAURU

Words written collectively

Music by
LAURENCE HENRY HICKS (*b.* 1912)

Moderato

mf Nau - ru bwi - e - ma, nga - ben - a ma au - we. Ma de - da - ro bwe do - gum, mo o - ta - ta bet eg - om. A - tsin nga - go bwi - en o - kor, a - ma ba - ga - du - gu E - po - a nga - bu - na ri nan or - re bet i - mur. A -

Officially adopted in 1968, when the country obtained independence.

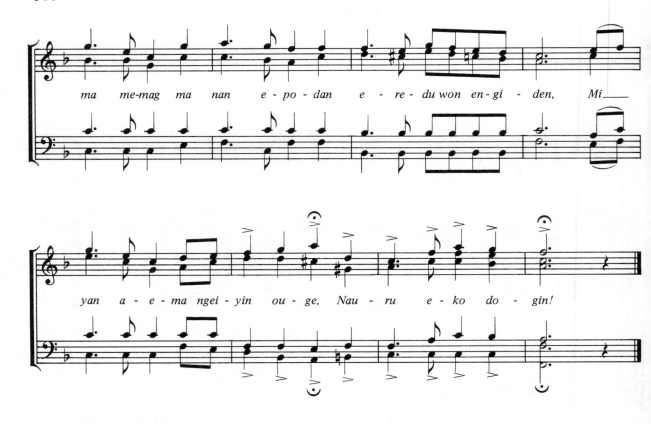

ma me-mag ma nan e-po-dan e-re-du won en-gi-den, Mi___

yan a-e-ma ngei-yin ou-ge, Nau-ru e-ko do-gin!

Translation

Nauru our homeland, the land we dearly love,
We all pray for you and we also praise your name.
Since long ago you have been the home of our great forefathers
And will be for generations yet to come.
We all join in together to honour your flag,
And we shall rejoice together and say;
    Nauru for evermore!

NEPAL

Words by
CHAKRAPANI CHALISE (1884-1959)

Music by
BAKHATBIR BUDHAPIRTHI (1857-1920)

Shri mân gum-bhi-ra ne-pâ-li pra-chan-da pra-tâ-pi bhu-pa-ti Shri pânch sar-kâr ma-hâ-râ-jâ-dhi-râ-ja ko sa-dâ ra-hos un-na-ti Ra-

-khun chi râ - yu ee - sha - le pra - jâ phai -

- li - yos pu - kâ - raun ja - ya pre - ma - le Hâ -

-mi ne - pâ - li bhâ - ee sâ - râ - le.

Free Translation

May glory crown you, courageous Sovereign, you,
the gallant Nepalese,
Shri Pansh Maharajadhiraja, our glorious ruler.
May he live for many years to come and may the
number of his subjects increase.
Let every Nepalese sing this with joy.

NETHERLANDS
Wilhelmus van Nassaouwe

Words by
PHILIP MARNIX van ST. ALDEGONDE (1540-1598)
Official Government translation

Composer unknown
Arr. by M.J. BRISTOW and W.L. REED

Allegro risoluto

1. Wil - hel - mus van Nas - sou - we Ben ick van Duyt - schen
1. Wil - liam of Nas - sau, scion of a Dutch and an - cient

Bloet, Den Va - der - land ghe - trou - we Blijf
line, I de - di - cate un - dy - ing Faith

ick tot in - den doet; Een Prin - ce
to this land of mine. A Prince I

Composer unknown: melody known from before 1572.
Song appeared in Valerius' "Gedenck-Clanck", 1626.
It has 15 verses in all.

van O - ran - gien Ben ick vry on - ver -
am, un - daunt - ed, Of O - range, e - ver

veert, Den Co - ninck van His -
free, To the King of Spain I've

pan - gien Heb ick al - tijt ghe - eert.
grant - ed A life - long loy - al - ty.

2. *Mijn schilt ende betrouwen*
   Zijt ghy, O Godt, mijn Heer,
   Op U soo wil ick bouwen,
   Verlaet my nimmermeer;
   Dat ick doch vroom mag blijven
   U dienaer t'aller stond,
   Die tyranny verdrijven,
   Die my mijn hert doorwondt.

2. A shield and my reliance,
   O God, Thou ever wert.
   I'll trust unto Thy guidance.
   O leave me not ungirt.
   That I may stay a pious
   Servant of Thine for aye,
   And drive the plagues the try us
   And tyranny away.

NEW ZEALAND

Words by
THOMAS BRACKEN (1843-1898)

Music by
JOHN JOSEPH WOODS (1849-1934)

1. God of na-tions at Thy_feet   In the bonds of   love_ we_ meet.
1. E   I-ho-a,   A-tu-a,   O nga I-wi!   Ma-tou-ra.

Hear our voi-ces,   we en-treat,   God de-fend our   Free_ Land.
A-ta wha-ka   ro-ngo-na;   Me a-ro-ha   no-a.

Guard Pa-ci-fic's   tri-ple_ star   From the shafts _of_   strife _ and _ war.
Ki-a hu-a   ko te_ pai;   Ki-a tau _ to   a-ta-whai;

324

Make her prais - es heard a - far, God de - fend New Zea - land.
Ma - na - a - ki - ti - a mai A - o - te - a - ro - a.

2. Men of every creed and race
   Gather here before Thy face,
   Asking Thee to bless this place,
   God defend our free land.
   From dissension, envy, hate
   And corruption guard our State,
   Make our country good and great,
   God defend New Zealand.

3. Peace, not war, shall be our boast,
   But, should foes assail our coast,
   Make us then a mighty host,
   God defend our free land.
   Lord of battles, in Thy might,
   Put our enemies to flight,
   Let our cause be just and right,
   God defend New Zealand.

4. Let our love for Thee increase,
   May Thy blessings never cease,
   Give us plenty, give us peace,
   God defend our free land.
   From dishonour and from shame,
   Guard our country's spotless name,
   Crown her with immortal fame,
   God defend New Zealand.

5. May our mountains ever be
   Freedom's ramparts on the sea,
   Make us faithful unto Thee,
   God defend our free land.
   Guide her in the nations' van,
   Preaching love and truth to man,
   Working out Thy glorious plan,
   God defend New Zealand.

2. *Ona mano tangata*
   Kiri whero, kiri ma,
   Iwi Maori Pakeha,
   Repeke katoa,
   Nei ka tono ko nga he
   Mau e whakaahu ke,
   Kia ora marire
   Aotearoa.

3. *Tona mana kia tu!*
   Tona kaha kia u;
   Tona rongo hei paku
   Ki te ao katoa,
   Aua rawa nga whawhai,
   Nga tutu a tata mai;
   Kia tupu nui ai .
   Aotearoa.

4. *Waiho tona takiwa*
   Ko te ao marama;
   Kia whiti tona ra
   Taiawhio noa.
   Ko te hae me te ngangau
   Meinga kia kore kau;
   Waiho i te rongo mau
   Aotearoa.

5. *Tona pai me toitu;*
   Tika rawa, pono pu;
   Tona noho, tana tu;
   Iwi no Ihoa.
   Kaua mona whakama;
   Kia hau te ingoa;
   Kia tu hei tauira;
   Aotearoa.

NICARAGUA

Words by
SOLOMÓN IBARRA MAYORGA (*b.* 1887)
English versification by
MARY ELIZABETH SHAW

Composer unknown
(Composed before 1821)

Sal - ve a ti Ni - ca - ra - gua en tu
Hail Ni - ca - ra - gua! the thun - der of

sue - - lo, ya no ru - ge la
can - - non Calls thy peo - ple no

voz___ del cañ - ón ni___ se ti - ñe con san - gre de her-
-lon - ger to war, And___ thy ban - ner, twin co - loured flies

The words formerly sung were replaced by these words in 1939 by a governmental decree.
By permission of J.B. Cramer & Co. Ltd.

NIGER

Words by
MAURICE ALBERT THIRIET (1906-1969)

Music by
ROBERT JACQUET (1896-1976) and
NICOLAS ABEL FRANÇOIS FRIONNET (*b.* 1911)

1. Au-près du grand Ni-ger puis-sant Qui rend la na-tu-re plus bel - le,

So - yons fiers et re-con - nais-sants De no-tre li-ber-té nou-vel - le.

E - vi-tons les vai - nes que-rel - les A-fin d'é-par-gner no-tre sang;

Niger became fully independent in 1960.
This National Anthem was approved by the National Assembly in July 1961.

Et que les glo-rieux ac-cents De no-tre ra-ce sans tu-

-tel - le S'é-lèvent dans un même é-lan Jus-

-qu'à ce ciel é-blou-is-sant Où veil - le son âme é-ter-

-nel - le Qui fe-ra le pa-ys plus grand.____ De-

CHORUS

Allegro

-bout Ni-ger: De - bout!___ Que no - tre œu - vre fé - conde Ra-

-jeu - nis-se le cœur de ce vieux con - ti - nent___ Et

que ce chant s'en - tende___ aux qua - tre coins du mon - de Com-

-me le cri d'un Peuple é - qui - table et vail - lant!___ De-

2. *Nous retrouvons dans nos enfants*
Toutes les vertus des Ancêtres:
Pour lutter dans tous les instants
Elles sont notre raison d'être.
Nous affrontons le fauve traître
A peine armés le plus souvent
Voulant subsister dignement
Sans detruire pour nous repaître.
Dans la steppe où chacun ressent
La soif, dans le Sahel brûlant,
Marchons, sans défaillance, en maîtres
Magnanimes et vigilants.

Translation by
T.M. Cartledge

1. By the waters of the mighty Niger
Which adds to the beauty of nature,
Let us be proud and grateful
For our new-won liberty.
Let us avoid vain quarrelling
So that our blood may be spared,
And may the glorious voice
Of our race, free from tutelage,
Rise unitedly, surging as from one man,
To the dazzling skies above
Where its eternal soul, watching over us,
Brings greatness to the country.

2. We find again in our children
All the virtues of our ancestors.
Such virtues are our inspiration
For fighting at every moment.
We confront ferocious and treacherous animals
Often scarcely armed,
Seeking to live in dignity,
Not slaying with a lust to kill.
In the steppe where all feel thirst,
In the burning desert,
Let us march tirelessly forward
As magnanimous and vigilant masters.

Chorus
Arise, Niger, arise! May our fruitful work
Rejuvenate the heart of this old continent,
And may this song resound around the world
Like the cry of a just and valiant people.
Arise, Niger, arise! On land and river
To the rhythm of the swelling drum-beats' sound
May we ever be united and may each one of us
Answer the call of this noble future that says to us, "Forward!"

NIGERIA

Words written collectively

Music by
BENEDICT ELIDE ODIASE (*b.* 1934)

1. A - rise, O Com-pa - triots, Ni - ge - ria's call o -
2. O God of cre - a - tion, Di - rect our no - ble

bey To serve our Fa - ther - land With __ love and strength and faith. The
cause; Guide Thou our Lead - ers right: Help our Youth the truth to know, In

la - bour of our he -roes past Shall ne - ver be in vain, To serve with heart and
love and hon - est - y to grow, And li - ving just and true, Great lof - ty heights at-

might __ One na - tion bound in free - dom, __ peace and u - ni - ty.
tain, __ To build a na - tion where peace __ and jus - tice __ reign.

Adopted 1978, replacing the Anthem composed in 1960.

NORWAY

Words by
BJØRNSTJERNE BJØRNSON (1832-1910)
Translation by
G.M. GATHORNE-HARDY

Music by
RIKARD NORDRAAK (1842-1866)

Adopted as the National Anthem in 1864, when first public recital was given on the fiftieth anniversary of the Norwegian constitution.

2. *Norske mann i hus og hytte,*
    Takk din store Gud!
    Landet ville han beskytte,
    Skjønt det mørkt så ut.
    Alt, hva fedrene har kjempet,
    Mødrene har grætt,
    Har den Herre stille lempet,
    Så vi vant vår rett,
    Har den Herre stille lempet,
    Så vi vant, vi vant vår rett.

3. *Ja, vi elsker dette landet,*
    Som det stiger frem
    Furet, værbitt over vannet,
    Med de tusen hjem!
    Og som fedres kamp har hevet
    Det av nød til seir,
    Også vi, når det blir krevet,
    For dets fred slår leir,
    Også vi, nar det blir krevet,
    For dets fred, dets fred slår leir!

2. Norseman, whatsoe'er thy station,
    Thank thy God, Whose power
    Willed and wrought the land's salvation
    In her darkest hour.
    All our mothers sought with weeping
    And our sires in fight,
    God has fashioned, in His keeping, { *bis. (repeating "we gained"*
    Till we gained our right.   { *the second time)*

3. Yes, we love with fond devotion
    This our land that looms
    Rugged, storm-scarred, o'er the ocean
    With her thousand homes.
    And, as warrior sires have made her
    Wealth and fame increase,
    At the call we too will aid her, { *bis. (repeating "to guard"*
    Armed to guard her peace.   { *the second time)*

OMAN

Author unknown

Composer unknown
Arr. (1972) by
RODNEY BASHFORD (*b.* 1917)

Muscat and Oman became Oman in 1970.
The anthem has been in use since 1972.

Ya Rabbana Ehfidh Lana Jalalat Al Sultan
Waashabi Fee Alawtan
Bialazy Walaman.

Walyadum Muoayadda Aahilan Momajjada.
Bilnufoosi Yuftda.

Ya Oman, Nahnoo Min Ahd Al Nabi
Awfiya Min Kiram Al Arabi.
Abshiry Qaboos Ja-a
Faltubarakhu Al Sama.

Wassidy Waltaqihi Bilduoaa.

Translation

O Lord, protect for us our Majesty the Sultan
And the people in our land,
With honour and peace.

May he live long, strong and supported,
Glorified be his leadership.
For him we shall lay down our lives.

O Oman, since the time of the Prophet
We are a dedicated people amongst the noblest Arabs.
Be happy! Qaboos has come
With the blessings of Heaven.

Be cheerful and commend him to the protection of your prayers.

PAKISTAN

Words by
ABU-AL-ASAR HAFEEZ JULLANDHURI
(1900-1982)

Music by
AHMED GHULAMALI CHAGLA
(1902-1953)
Arr. by **BRYSON GERRARD**

Music officially accepted as National Anthem, December 1953.
Words officially accepted as text of National Anthem, August 1954.

Tar - ju - ma - ne ma - zi - sha - ne hal ja - ne is - taq - bal

Say - yai, khu - dae zul ja - lal.

Free Translation

1. Blessed be the sacred land,
   Happy be the bounteous realm,
   Symbol of high resolve,
   Land of Pakistan.
   Blessed be thou citadel of faith.

2. The Order of this Sacred Land
   Is the might of the brotherhood of the people.
   May the nation, the country, and the State
   Shine in glory everlasting.
   Blessed be the goal of our ambition.

3. This flag of the Crescent and the Star
   Leads the way to progress and perfection,
   Interpreter of our past, glory of our present,
   Inspiration of our future,
   Symbol of Almighty's protection.

PANAMA
Himno Istmeño

Words by
JERÓNIMO de la OSSA (1847-1907)
English versification by
SEBASTIAN SHAW

Music by
JORGE SANTOS (1870-1941)
Arr. by MARTIN SHAW

Marziale

CHORUS f energico

Al - can - za - mos por fin___ la vic -
Fi - nal vic - to - ry honoured then our

- to - ria, en el cam - po fe - liz de la u - nión, Con ar -
sto - ry, When at last we gained u - nion's fair field. Shin - ing

- dien - tes ful - go - res de glo - ria se ilu -
bright in the blaze of her glo - ry, Now be -

This anthem was used for the first time on 4 November, 1903, when the people carried the flag of the new Republic through the streets of the capital. It was officially adopted in 1925.

-mi - na la nue - va Na - ción_____ Con ar-dien - tes ful-go - res de
-hold, the new nation is re - vealed!_____ Shin - ing bright in the blaze of her

glo - ria se ilu - mi - na la nue - va Na - ción.
glo - ry, Now be - hold, the new nation is re - vealed!

Fine

VERSE
p dolce

1. Es pre - ci - so cu-brir con un ve - lo, del pa-
1. We re - joice that, the Cal - va - ry end - ed, And the

p dolce

-sa - do el cal-va - rio y la cruz,_____ y que a-
Cross be - ing veiled in the past,_____ Gen - tle

2. *En tu suelo cubierto de flores,*
A los besos del tibio terral,
Terminaron guerreros fragores,
Sólo reina el amor fraternal.
Adelante la pica y la pala,
Al trabajo sin más dilación:
Y seremos asi prez y gala
De este mundo feraz de Colón.

2. From your soil, where gay flowers are greeted
   By the warmth of the breezes' caress,
   Far the clamours of war have retreated;
   Love fraternal your future will bless.
   Then with spade and with hammer, untiring,
   To his task let each man set his hand;
   So, to honour and glory aspiring,
   Shall we prosper Columbus' fair land.

PAPUA NEW GUINEA

Words and music by
THOMAS SHACKLADY (*b.* 1917)

1. O a - rise all you sons of this land, Let us
2. Now give thanks to the good Lord a - bove For His

sing of our joy to be free, Prais - ing God and re - joic - ing to
kind - ness, His wis - dom and love For this land of our fa - thers so

be Pa - pu - a New Gui - nea.
free, Pa - pu - a New Gui - nea.

Words and music by Chief Inspector Thomas Shacklady, Bandmaster of the Royal Papua New Guinea
Constabulary. Adopted in 1975, when the country became independent.

CHORUS

Shout our name from the moun - tains to seas - Pa - pu -
Shout a - gain for the whole world to hear - Pa - pu -

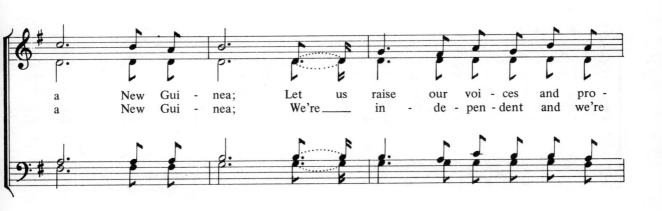

a New Gui - nea; Let us raise our voi - ces and pro -
a New Gui - nea; We're___ in - de - pen - dent and we're

rall. _ _ _ _ _ _ _ _ _ _ _ _ _ _

claim Pa - pu - a ___ New Gui - nea.
free, PA - PU - A ___ NEW GUI - NEA.

PARAGUAY

Words by
FRANCISCO ESTEBAN ACUÑA de FIGUEROA
(1791-1862)
Versified English version by
T.M. CARTLEDGE

Music by
FRANCISCO JOSÉ DEBALI (1791-1859)
Transcribed by
REMBERTO GIMÉNEZ

A los pue-blos de A-mé-ri-ca in-faus - to, Tres cen-
Once the lands of A-me-ri-ca, sad and op-pressed, 'Neath a

-tu-rias un ___ ce-tro o-pri-mió, Más un
scep-tre for three cen-tu-ries re-mained. But one

dí - a so-ber-bia sur-gien - - -
day, with their pas-sion a-ris - - -

Adopted as National Anthem, 1846.
This present arrangement was declared the official version in May 1934. There are seven verses in all.
Francisco de Figueroa also wrote the words of the Uruguayan National Anthem.
Francisco Debali also composed the music for the Uruguayan National Anthem.

PERU

Words by
JOSÉ de la TORRE UGARTE (1786-1831)

Music by
JOSÉ BERNARDO ALCEDO (1788-1878)
Arr. by HENRY COLEMAN

Words and music chosen as result of a competition for a national anthem promoted by General San Martín in 1821. They were declared official on 12 February, 1913.
There were originally six verses, but the first verse only is now sung.

-te - mos al vo - to so - lem - ne que la Pa - tria al E - ter-no̲e-le-

-vó___ que fal - te - mos al vo - to so - lem - ne que_ la

Pa - tria̲al E - ter - no̲e-le - vó___ que fal - te - mos al vo - to so-

-lem - ne que_ la Pa - tria̲al E - ter - no-e-le - vó.___

Fine

VERSE

1. Lar - go tiem - po_el pe - rua - no_o-pri - mi - do la_o - mi -

- no - sa ca-de - na_arras-tró;_____ con-de - na - do_a u-na cruel ser - vi -

-dum - - bre, lar-go tiem-po lar-go tiem-po lar - go

tiem-po_en si-len - cio gi - mió._____ Mas a - pe - nas el gri - to sa -

Free Translation

CHORUS We are free; let us always be so,
      And let the sun rather deny its light
      Than that we should fail the solemn vow
      Which our Country raised to God.

VERSE   For a long time the Peruvian, oppressed,
      Dragged the ominous chain;
      Condemned to cruel serfdom,
      For a long time he moaned in silence.
      But as soon as the sacred cry of
      Freedom! was heard on his coasts
      He shakes the indolence of the slave,
      He raises his humiliated head.

PHILIPPINES

Original Spanish words by
JOSÉ PALMA (1876-1903)
New Tagalog translation by
FELIPE P. de LEON
English translation by M.A.L. LANE

Music by
JULIAN FELIPE (1861-194

First performed in conjunction with the reading of the Act of Proclamation of Independence, 12 June, 1898
The words were written in 1899.

Sa man - lu - lu - pig Di ka pa - si - si - il.
Ne'er shall in - va - ders Tram-ple thy sa - cred shore.

3. Sa da - gat at bun - dok, Sa si - moy at sa
3. Ev - er with - in thy skies and through thy clouds And

la - ngit mong bug - haw, May di - lag ang tu - la At
o'er thy hills and sea Do we be - hold the ra - diance,

a - wit sa pag la - yang mi - na - ma -
Feel the throb Of glo - rious lib - er -

360

Original words written in Spanish

1. *Tierra adorada.*
    hija del sol de Oriente
    su fuego ardiente
    en ti latiendo está.

2. *Tierra de amores,*
    del heróismo cuna,
    los invasores
    no te hollarán jamás.

3. *En tu azul cielo, en tus auras,*
    en tus montes y en tu mar
    esplende y late el poema
    de tu amada libertad.

4. *Tu pabellón que en las lides*
    la victoria iluminó
    no verá nunca apagados
    sus estrellas ni su sol.

5. *Tierra de dichas, de sol y amores,*
    en tu regazo dulce es vivir;
    es una gloria para tus hijos,
    cuando te ofenden, por ti morir.

Repeat Verses 1 & 2.

POLAND

Words by
JÓZEF WYBICKI (1747-1822)
Translation by
MARTIN SHAW

Composer unknown

Allegretto vivace

1. *Jeszc - ze Pol - ska nie zgi-ne - ta,__ kie - dy my zy -*
1. Po - land still is ours for ev - er,__ Long as Poles re -

- je - my, co nam ob - ca prze - moc zie - ta,__
- main;__ Chains the foe bound on her nev - er__

szab - la od - bie - rze - my. Marsz, marsz, Da - brow - ski;
Shall the foe re - tain.__ On! On! Da - bru - ski!* from

This song, first sung in 1795, was a favourite with the Polish Legions in the Napoleonic wars. It has been sung all over Poland since 1912; in 1927 it was authorised as its National Anthem by the new Polish republican government.

* General Dabruski (1755-1818) commanded the Polish Legions.

General Wybicki was among those who organised and led the Legions. He was also a poet and a member of the Polish Parliament.

The melody is the same as that of the National Anthem of Yugoslavia.

2. *Przejdziem Wisłę, przejdziem Wartę,*
   będziem Polakami,
   dał nam przykład Bonaparte
   jak zwyciężać mamy.
       Marsz, marsz, Dąbrowski

2. Vistula and Wartar over,
   Poles we'll ever be;
   And from Bonaparte discover
   Paths to victory.
       On! On! etc.

3. *Jak Czarniecki do Poznania*
   po szwedzkim zaborze,
   dla ojczyzny ratowania
   wrócim się przez morze.
       Marsz, marsz, Dąbrowski

3. When the Swede had forged our chain,
   The Fatherland to save,
   Czarniecki, Poznan town to gain,
   Plunged into the wave.
       On! On! etc.

PORTUGAL

Words by
HENRIQUE LOPES de MENDONÇA (1856-1931)

Music by
ALFREDO KEIL (1850-1907)
Arr. by HENRY COLEMAN

1. Herois do mar, no - bre po - vo, Na - ção va - len - te,___ i - mor - tal, Le - van - tai ho - je de no - vo O es - plen - dor___ de Por - tu - gal!___ En - tre as bru - mas da me - mó - ria, Ó

First played January 1890, approved as the National Anthem in 1910.

Pá - tria lu - tar!_____ Con-tra os ca-nhões mar-char, mar-char!

2. Desfralda a invicta bandeira
    À luz viva do teu céu!
    Brade à Europa à terra inteira:
    Portugal não pereceu!
    Beija o solo teu jucundo
    O Oceano a rugir d'amor;
    E o teu braço vencedor
    Deu novos mundos ao mundo!

Estribilho   Às armas, às armas!
              Sobre a terra, sobre o mar,
              Às armas, às armas!
              Pela pátria lutar!
              Contra os canhões marchar,
                  Marchar!

3. Saudai o sol que desponta
    Sobre um ridente porvir;
    Seja o eco de uma afronta
    O sinal do ressurgir.
    Ráios dessa aurora forte
    São como beijos de mãe
    Que nos guardam, nos sustêm
    Contra as injúrias da sorte.

Estribilho   Às armas, às armas!
              Sobre a terra, sobre o mar,
              Às armas, às armas!
              Pela pátria lutar!
              Contra os canhões marchar,
                  Marchar!

Official English Paraphrase

1. Heroes of the sea, noble race
    Valiant and immortal nation,
    Now is the hour to raise up on high once more
    Portugal's splendour.
    From out of the mists of memory,
    Oh Homeland, we hear the voices
    Of your great forefathers
    That shall lead you on to victory!

CHORUS To arms, to arms
        On land and sea!
        To arms, to arms
        To fight for our Homeland!
        To march against the enemy guns!

2. Unfurl the unconquerable flag
    In the bright light of your sky!
    Cry out to all Europe and the whole world
    That Portugal has not perished.
    Your happy land is kissed
    By the Ocean that murmurs with love.
    And your conquering arm
    Has given new worlds to the world!

CHORUS To arms, to arms
        On land and sea!
        To arms, to arms
        To fight for our Homeland!
        To march against the enemy guns!

3. Salute the Sun that rises
    On a smiling future:
    Let the echo of an insult be
    The signal for our revival.
    The rays of that powerful dawn
    Are like a mother's kisses
    That protect us and support us
    Against the insults of fate.

CHORUS To arms, to arms
        On land and sea!
        To arms, to arms
        To fight for our Homeland!
        To march against the enemy guns!

QATAR

No words

ROMANIA

Words by various authors
Adapted from CIPRIAN PORUMBESCU's
Original version

Music by
CIPRIAN PORUMBESCU (1853-1883)

1. Trei cu - lori cu-nosc pe lu – me, A - min-tind de-un brav po -
2. Mul – te se – co - le lup-ta – ră Stră-bu-nii noș - tri e -
3. Ro – șu, gal – ben și al - bas-tru Es-te-al nos - tru tri-co -

por, Ce-i vi-teaz, cu vechi re – nu – me, În lup-tă tri-um-fă –
roi, Să tră-im stă-pîni în ţa – ră Zi-di-tori ai lu-mii
lor, Se î – nal – ţă ca un as – tru, Glo-ri-o - sul meu po-

tor, Ce-i vi-teaz, cu vechi re-nu – me, În lup-tă tri-um-fă - tor.
noi, Să tră-im stă-pîni în ţa – ră, Zi-di-tori ai lu-mii noi.
por, Se î – nal-ţă ca un as-tru, Glo-ri-o-sul meu po-por.

Adopted October 29, 1977.

This replaces the Anthem composed in 1953.
Ciprian Porumbescu also wrote the music of the Albanian National Anthem.

4. Sîntem un popor în lume
    Strîns unit şi muncitor,
    Liber, cu un nou renume   } *(repeat)*
    Şi un ţel cutezător.

5. Azi partidul ne uneşte
    Şi pe plaiul românesc
    Socialismul se clădeşte   } *(repeat)*
    Prin elan muncitoresc.

6. Pentru-a patriei onoare,
    Vrăjmaşii-n luptă-i zdrobim.
    Cu alte neamuri sub soare,   } *(repeat)*
    Demn, în pace, să trăim.

7. Iar tu, Românie mîndră,
    Tot mereu să dăinuieşti
    Şi în comunista eră   } *(repeat)*
    Ca o stea să străluceşti.

Translation by Andrei Bantas

1. With three colours I'm acquainted
    Which recall a gallant race —
    Since old times by glory sainted } *(repeat)*
    Battles has it won apace.

2. For long ages our forefathers
    Have this gallant flag unfurled
    So we may the land's fruit gather, } *(repeat)*
    Building here the future's world.

3. This tricolour flag of ours
    Flutters crimson, yellow, blue,
    Like a star in skyey bowers } *(repeat)*
    Rise my people, brave and true.

4. In this world we are a nation
    Keen on work and of one soul,
    Free and with new reputation, } *(repeat)*
    Sharing one ambitious goal.

5. Now united by our Party;
    In Romania's meads and fields,
    Our work is hard and hearty, } *(repeat)*
    Building Socialism its yield.

6. For the homeland's greater glory
    We crush enemies at fight,
    But we'd share a peaceful story } *(repeat)*
    With all peoples in proud light.

7. Proud Romania, now dearer,
    Live forever in fine light!
    In the Communist new era
    Like a star you must shine bright! } *(repeat)*

RWANDA

Based on an old Rwandan Folk tune by a
group of Rwandans (Abanyuramatwi)*
Arr. by W.L. REED

Moderato maestoso

1. Rwa - nda rwa-cu, Rwa-nda gi-hu-gu cya - mbya - ye,
2. I - mpu-ndu ni zi-vu-ge mu Rwa-nda ho - se:
3. Ba - vu - ka Rwa-nda mwe-se mu-vu z'i - mpu-ndu,
4. Ni - mu-cyo du-si-ngi-z'I-be-nde-ra rya - cu.

con 8va ad lib.

nda - ku-ra-ta-n'i-shya-ka n'u - bu - twa - li.
Re - pu-bu-li-ka ya-ku y'u - bu - ha - ke,
De - mo-ka-ra-si ya-rwo i - ra - ga - nje.
A - ra-ka-ba-ho na Pre - zi - da wa - cu.

I - yo ni-bu-ts'i-bi gwi wa-gi - ze ku-ge-z'u-bu,
u - bu-ko-lo-ni-ze bwa-gi-ye nk'i - fu-n'i-he-ze.
Twa-yi-ha-ra-ni-ye rwo-se twe-s'u - ko tu-nga-na.
Ba-ra-ka-ba-hw'a-ba-tu-ra-ge b'i - ki Gi-hu-gu.

This anthem was adopted by the National Assembly and sanctioned by the President of the Republic on
11 December, 1962, the year when the country became independent.
* This was the name of a Choral Society.

molto rit.

- ho - ro, mu ku - li,   mu   bwi - ge - nge   no mu   bwu - mvi - ka - ne.
- ho - ro, mu ku - li,   mu   bwi - ge - nge   no mu   bwu - mvi - ka - ne.
- ho - ro, mu ku - li,   mu   bwi - ge - nge   no mu   bwu - mvi - ka - ne.
- ho - ro, mu ku - li,   mu   bwi - ge - nge   no mu   bwu - mvi - ka - ne.

molto rit.

Translation

1. My Rwanda, land that gave me birth,
   Fearlessly, tirelessly, I boast of you!
   When I recall your achievements to this very day,
   I praise the pioneers who have brought in our unshakeable Republic.
   Brothers all, sons of this Rwanda of ours,
   Come rise up all of you,
   > Let us cherish her in peace and in truth,
   > In freedom and in harmony!

2. Let the victory drums beat throughout all Rwanda!
   The Republic has swept away feudal bondage.
   Colonialism has faded away like a worn-out shoe.
   Democracy take root!
   Through you we have chosen our own rulers.
   People of Rwanda, old and young, citizens all,
   > Let us cherish her in peace and in truth,
   > In freedom and in harmony!

3. Home-born Rwandans all, beat the victory drums!
   Democracy has triumphed in our land.
   All of us together we have striven for it arduously.
   Together we have decreed it— Tutsi, Twa, Hutu, with other racial elements,
   This hard-won Independence of ours,
   Let us all join to build it up!
   > Let us cherish it in peace and in truth,
   > In freedom and in harmony!

4. Come let us extol our Flag!
   Long live our President, long live the citizens of our land!
   Let this be our aim, people of Rwanda:
   To stand on our own feet, in our own right, by our own means.
   Let us promote unity and banish fear.
   Let us go forward together in Rwanda.
   > Let us cherish her in peace and in truth,
   > In freedom and in harmony!

SAINT KITTS and NEVIS

Words and music by
KENRICK ANDERSON GEORGES (*b.* 1955)
Arr. by W.L. REED

Adopted in 1983.

God in all our strug - gles, Saint Kitts and Ne - vis
sword nor spear can con - quer, For God will sure de -

be A Na - tion bound to - ge - ther With a com-mon des - ti -
fend. His bless - ings shall for e - ver To pos - ter - i - ty ex -

FINE

D.S. al Fine

ny. 2. As stal - warts we stand, For
tend.

SAINT LUCIA

Words by
CHARLES JESSE (*b.* 1897)

Music by
LETON FELIX THOMAS (*b.* 1926)
Arr. by W.L. REED

1. Sons and daugh-ters of St. Lu-cia, Love the land that gave us birth,
2. Gone the times when na-tions bat-tled For this 'He-len of the West',
3. May the good Lord bless our is-land, Guard her sons from woe and harm!

Land of bea-ches, hills and val-leys, Fair-est isle of — all the earth.
Gone the days when strife and dis-cord Dimmed her chil-dren's toil and rest.
May our peo-ple live u-ni-ted, Strong in soul and — strong in arm!

Where-so-ev-er you may roam, — Love, oh — love your is-land home!
Dawns at last a brigh-ter day, — Stret-ches out a glad new way.
Jus-tice, Truth and Cha-ri-ty, — Our i-deal for e-ver be!

Originally adopted in 1967 on achieving Statehood, and again in 1979 when becoming independent.

SAINT VINCENT and THE GRENADINES

Words by
PHYLLIS JOYCE McCLEAN PUNNETT (*b.* 1917)

Music by
JOEL BERTRAM MIGUEL (*b.* 1938)

Maestoso

f

1. Saint Vin-cent! Land so beau-ti-ful, With __ joy-ful hearts we
2. Hai-roun! Our fair and bless-ed Isle, Your __ moun-tains high, so
3. Our lit-tle sis-ter is-lands are Those __ gems, the love-ly

cresc.

pledge to thee Our loy-al-ty and love, and vow To __ keep you e - ver
clear and green, Are home to me, though I may stray, A __ ha-ven, calm, se -
Gren-a-dines, Up - on their seas and gold-en sands The __ sun-shine e - ver

CHORUS

ff *mp*

free. _____
rene. _____ What - e'er the fu-ture brings, Our faith will __ see us
beams. _____

rall.
cresc.

keep us

ff

through. _____ May peace reign from shore to shore, And God bless and keep us true.

Originally adopted in 1969 on achieving Statehood, and again in 1979 when becoming independent.

SAN MARINO

No words

Music by
FEDERICO CONSOLO (1841-1906)

Adopted in 1894. The music is based on a tenth century chorale from a breviary in the Biblioteca Laurenziana.

SÃO TOMÉ and PRÍNCIPE

Arr. by W.L. REED

SAUDI ARABIA

No words

Music by
ABDUL RAHMAN AL-KHATEEB (*b.* 1923)

First performed 1947, adopted 1950.

SENEGAL

Words by
LEOPOLD SÉDAR SENGHOR (*b.* 1906)

Music by
HERBERT PEPPER (*b.* 1912)

1. Fin-cez tous vos Ko-ras, Frap-pez les ba-la-fons, Le

Lion rouge a ru-gi Le Domp-teur de la brousse d'un

bond s'est é-lan-cé Dis-si-pant les tén-è-bres. So-

This National Anthem was adopted in 1960, when the country became independent.
The words are by the President, Leopold Sédar Senghor.
Herbert Pepper also wrote the music for the National Anthem of the Central African Republic.
Harp-Lute of the Senegalese Griots.

U - nis - sons la mer et les sour - ces, U - nis - sons la

steppe et la fo-rêt. Sa-lut Af-ri-que mè-re. -lut A-fri-que mère.

2. *Sénégal, toi le fils de l'écume du Lion,*
   Toi surgi de la nuit au galop des chevaux,
   Rends-nous, oh! rends-nous l'honneur de nos Ancêtres,
   Splendides comme ébène et forts comme le muscle
   Nous disons droits— l'épée n'a pas une bavure.

3. *Sénégal, nous faisons nôtre ton grand dessein:*
   Rassembler les poussins à l'abri des milans
   Pour en faire, de l'Est à l'Ouest, du Nord au Sud,
   Dressé, un même peuple, un peuple sans couture
   Mais un peuple tourné vers tous les vents du monde.

4. *Sénégal, comme toi, comme tous nos héros,*
   Nous serons durs sans haine et des deux bras ouverts.
   L'épée, nous la mettrons dans la paix du fourreau,
   Car le travail sera notre arme et la parole.
   Le Bantou est un frère, et l'Arabe et le Blanc.

5. *Mais que si l'ennemi incendie nos frontières*
    Nous serons tous dressés et les armes au poing:
    Un Peuple dans sa foi défiant tous les malheurs,
    Les jeunes et les vieux, les hommes et les femmes.
    La Mort, oui! Nous disons la Mort, mais pas la honte.

Free Translation by
Elizabeth P. Coleman

1. Sound, all of you, your Koras,
    Beat the drums,
    The red Lion has roared,
    The Tamer of the bush with one leap has rushed forward
    Scattering the gloom.
            Light on our terrors,
            Light on our hopes.
    Arise, brothers, Africa behold united.

Chorus

Shoulder to shoulder,
O people of Senegal, more than brothers to me, arise!
Unite the sea and the springs,
Unite the steppe and the forest.
Hail, mother Africa,
Hail, mother Africa.

2. Senegal, thou son of the Lion,
    Arise in the night with great speed,
    Restore, oh, restore to us the honour of our ancestors,
    Magnificent as ebony and strong as muscles,
    We are a straight people—the sword has no fault.

3. Senegal, we make your great design our own:
    To gather the chicks, sheltering them from kites,
    To make from them, from East to West, from North to South,
    A people rising as one, in seamless unity,
    Yet a people facing all the winds of the earth.

4. Senegal, like thee, like all our heroes,
    We will be stern without hatred, and with open arms.
    The sword we will put peacefully in its sheath,
    For work and words will be our weapon.
    The Bantu is our brother, the Arab, and the White man too.

5. But if the enemy violates our frontiers,
    We will all be ready, weapons in our hands;
    A people in its faith defying all evil;
    Young and old, men and women,
    Death, yes! but not dishonour.

SEYCHELLES

Music by
PIERRE DASTROS - GÈZE (*b.* 1925)
Arr. by W.L. REED

ords written collectively

dopted in 1978.

Translation

1. With courage and discipline we have broken all barriers.
   With the tiller in our hands, we will always remain brothers.
   Never, never shall we cease struggling.
   Death rather than to live in slavery!
   Never, never shall we cease struggling.
   Equality for all of us! Freedom for ever!

CHORUS Rise, free men!
   Proud Seychellois, our doors are open.
   Our path is traced,
   Our sun has risen,
   We will not turn back.
   Rise, free men!
   Rise, Seychellois!
   Let us remain in unity and liberty.

2. With dignity we must cultivate our land,
   With determination we must exploit our seas.
   Let us for ever march together
   To harvest all we have planted.
   Let us for ever march together,
   Fraternity in our hearts, to the future ahead of us.

CHORUS

SIERRA LEONE

Words by
CLIFFORD NELSON FYLE (*b.* 1933)

Music by
JOHN JOSEPH AKAR (1927-1975)
Arr. by HENRY COLEMAN

1. High we ex-alt__ thee, realm of the free; Great is the love__ we have for__ thee; Firm-ly u-nit-ed e-ver we stand, Sing-ing thy praise, O__ nat-ive__ land. We raise up our hearts and our

Written and composed in 1961 and adopted as the National Anthem when the country achieved independence on 27 April, 1961.

voic - es on high, the hills and the val-leys re - e - cho our cry;

Bless-ing and peace be e-ver thine own, Land that we love, our_ Sier-ra Le-one.

2. One with a faith that wisdom inspires,
One with a zeal that never tires;
Ever we seek to honour thy name,
Ours is the labour, thine the fame.
We pray that no harm on thy children may fall,
That blessing and peace may descend on us all;
So may we serve thee ever alone,
Land that we love, our Sierra Leone.

3. Knowledge and truth our forefathers spread,
Mighty the nations whom they led;
Mighty they made thee, so too may we
Show forth the good that is ever in thee.
We pledge our devotion, our strength and our might,
Thy cause to defend and to stand for thy right;
All that we have be ever thine own,
Land that we love, our Sierra Leone.

SINGAPORE
Majulah Singapura

Words and music by
ZUBIR SAID (*b.* 1907)
Arr. by HENRY COLEMAN

Ma-ri ki - ta ra'- yat Si-nga-pu-ra sa-ma sa-ma mĕ-nu-ju ba-ha-gi - a. Chi-ta chi--ta ki-ta yang mu-li-a Ber-ja-ya Si-nga-pu - ra!

For Royal Salute play from * to *

First performed September, 1958. It became very popular and when the country became self-governing on 3 June, 1959, it was decided to make it the National Anthem. It was officially adopted as such by the Legislative Assembly on 30 November, 1959.

Free Translation

Let us, the people of Singapore, together march
forward towards happiness. Our noble aspiration
is to see Singapore achieve success.
Let us unite in a new spirit. We all pray:
"May Singapore Progress", "May Singapore Progress".

SOLOMON ISLANDS

Words by
PANAPASA BALEKANA (*b.* 1929) and
MATILA BALEKANA (*b.* 1932)

Music by
PANAPASA BALEKANA (*b.* 1929)

Chosen as the result of a competition, and first sung on Independence Day, July 7, 1978.

SOMALIA

No words

Music by
GIUSEPPE BLANC (1886-1969)
Arranged from band score by
W. L. REED

Adopted in 1960.

SOUTH AFRICA
Die Stem van Suid-Afrika
(The Call of South Africa)

Words by
CORNELIS JACOB LANGENHOVEN
(1873-1932)

Music by
MARTHINUS LOURENS de VILLIERS
(1885-1977)

Adopted in 1936; English version adopted in 1952, revised 1959.

with emphasis

a tempo

kran - se___ ant - woord gee, Deur ons vér ver - la - te
hoop op___ wat sal wees, In ons wil en werk en
e - choing crags re - sound; From our plains where creak - ing
glo - ry___ of our past; In our will, our work, our

vlak - tes met die kreun van os - se - wa___ Ruis die
wan - del, van ons wieg tot aan ons graf___ Deel geen
wag - ons cut their trails in - to the earth___ Calls the
striv - ing, from the cra - dle to the grave___ There's no

stem van ons ge - lief - de, van ons land Suid - A - fri -
an - der land ons lief - de, trek geen an - der___ trou ons
spi - rit of our Coun - try, of the land that___ gave us
land that shares our lov - ing, and no bond that___ can en -

3. *In die songloed van ons somer, in ons winternag se kou,*
   In die lente van ons liefde, in die lanfer van ons rou,
   By die klink van huw'liks-klokkies, by die kluitklap op die kis—
   Streel jou stem ons nooit verniet nie, weet jy waar jou kinders is.
   Op jou roep sê ons nooit nee nie, sê ons altyd, altyd ja:
   Om te lewe, on te sterwe-ja, ons kom, Suid-Afrika.

4. *Op U Almag vas vertrouend het ons vadere gebou:*
   Skenk ook ons die krag, o Here! om te handhaaf en te hou—
   Dat die erwe van ons vaad're vir ons kinders erwe bly:
   Knegte van die Allerhoogste, teen die hele wêreld vry.
   Soos ons vadere vertrou het, leer ook ons vertrou, o Heer—
   Met ons land en met ons nasie sal dit wel wees, God regeer.

Translation

3. In the golden warmth of summer, in the chill of winter's air,
   In the surging life of springtime, in the autumn of despair;
   When the wedding bells are chiming or when those we love depart,
   Thou dost know us for thy children and dost take us to thy heart.
   Loudly peals the answering chorus: We are thine, and we shall stand,
   Be it life or death, to answer to thy call, beloved land.

4. In Thy power, Almighty, trusting, did our fathers build of old;
   Strengthen then, O Lord, their children to defend, to love, to hold —
   That the heritage they gave us for our children yet may be:
   Bondsmen only to the Highest and before the whole world free.
   As our fathers trusted humbly, teach us, Lord, to trust Thee still:
   Guard our land and guide our people in Thy way to do Thy will.

SPAIN
Marcha Real

No words

Composer unknown
Arr. by MARTIN SHAW

This anthem, the *Marcha Real,* dates from 3 September, 1770, when it was declared by Royal Decree of Carlos III as the Spanish Royal March. In July 1942 General Franco issued a decree declaring it as the national hymn. There are no official words, though various writers have written verses at different times.

SRI LANKA

Words and music by
ANANDA SAMARAKONE (1911-1962)
Arr. by **SURYA SENA**

Adopted in 1952.

2. *Obave apa vidya obamaya apa sathya*
   ..... obave apa shakti
   apa hada thula bhakti oba apa āloke
   apage anuprane oba apa jeevana ve
   apa muktiya obave

3. *Nava jēēvana demine nithina apa*
   pubudu karan māthā
   Gnana vēērya vadavamina ragena yanu
   mana jaya bhōōmi karā
   Eka mavekuge daru kala bavinā
   yamu yamu wee nopamā
   Prema vadamu sama bheda durara
   　　　　　Namō Namō Māthā

Free Translation by C.W.W. Kannangara

Mother Lanka— we worship Thee!
Plenteous in prosperity, Thou,
Beauteous in grace and love,
Laden with corn and luscious fruit
And fragrant flowers of radiant hue,
Giver of life and all good things,
Our land of joy and victory,
Receive our grateful praise sublime,
Lanka! we worship Thee.

Thou gavest us Knowledge and Truth,
Thou art our strength and inward faith,
Our light divine and sentient being,
Breath of life and liberation.
Grant us, bondage free, inspiration.
Inspire us for ever.
In wisdom and strength renewed,
Ill-will, hatred, strife all ended,
In love enfolded, a mighty nation
Marching onward, all as one,
Lead us, Mother, to fullest freedom.

SUDAN

Words by
AHMAD MUHAMMAD SALIH (1896-1971)
English versification by
T.M. CARTLEDGE

Music by
AHMAD MARJAN (1905-1974)
Arr. by T.M. CARTLEDGE

Nah - nu__ Djun - dul - lah   Djun - dul - wa - tan.
We are the ar - my of God   and   of   our land,

In ____ Da A   Da   Il Fi - da   Lam Na - khun.
We shall ne - ver fail, called to make sac - ri - fice.

Na - ta - had - dal Maut   End - al - mi - han.
Wheth-er brav - ing death,   hard - ship   or pain,

Officially adopted in 1956.

Nash - ta Ril___ Madjd Bi Agh - la - tha - man.
We for glo - ry give our lives as the price.

Ha - thi -hil Ard La - na! Fal - ya - ish Su - da - nu - na,
This our land, our Su-dan, Long may she now live, we pray,

A - la - man Bayn Al U - mam.
Show - ing all na - tions the way.

Ya Be - nis - su - dan,   Ha - tha - ram - zu - kum:
Sons of the Su - dan,   sum - moned now to serve.

Yah Mi - lul - eb,   Wa Yah - mi Ar - da - kum.
Shoul - der - ing the task   our coun - try to pre - serve.

SURINAM

Dutch words by
CORNELIS ATSES HOEKSTRA (1852-1911)
Sranan version by
HENRY de ZIEL (1916-1975)

Music by
JOHANNES CORSTIANUS de PUY (1835-1924)
Arr. by HENRY COLEMAN

God zij met ons Su - ri - na - me! Hij ver-
O - po kon - dre - man oen o - po Sra - nan-

-heff' ons heer - lijk land! Hoe wij hier ook sa - men
-gron e ka - ri oen. Wans o - pe ta - ta ko-

kwa - men, aan zijn grond zijn wij ver - pand. Wer-kend
-mo - po, wi moe se - ti kon - dré boen. Stré de

The music was written in 1876, the words in 1893.

hou-den w'in ge-dach-ten, Recht en waar-heid ma-ken vrij. Al wat
f'stré wi no sa fre-de Ga-do de wi fe-si-man. E-ri

goed is te be-trach-ten, Dat geeft aan ons land waar-dij.
li-bi té na de-de, wi sa fe-ti gi Sra-nan.

Translation by T.M. Cartledge
(from the Dutch)

God be with our Surinam!
May He glorify our beautiful land!
However we came together here,
We are pledged to your soil.
As we work. let us remember
That justice and truth make us free.
Practising all that is good
Will make our country a worthy land.

SWAZILAND

Words by
ANDREASE ENOKE FANYANA SIMELANE
(b. 1934)

Music by
DAVID KENNETH RYCROFT
(b. 1924)

This anthem was selected from some 100 entries in a National Anthem competition, when the country attained independence on 6 September, 1968.

The composer, Mr. David Rycroft, is a Lecturer in Bantu Languages at the University of London, and author of the first si Swati-English dictionary. His anthem was composed after ethnomusicological fieldwork in Swaziland and is a compromise between Swazi and Western music. The Swazi musical tradition in unusual in that there are no drums. The stress is on choral dance-songs, with intricate polyphony, rather than on the more usual rhythmic subtleties found elsewhere in Africa.

412

*'*c*' is a dental click consonant.

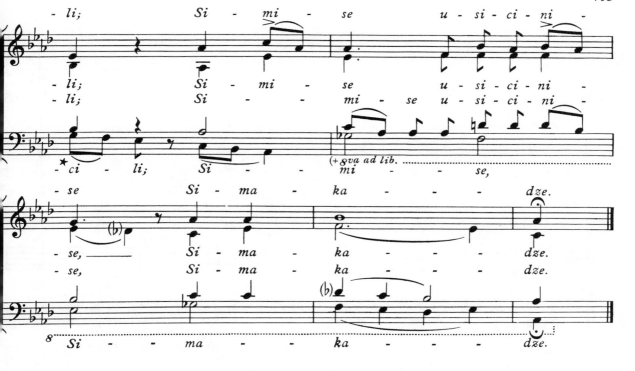

Free Translation

O God, bestower of the blessings of the Swazi;
We are thankful for all our good fortune,
We give praise and thanks for our King
And for our country, its hills and rivers.
Bless those in authority in Swaziland,
Thou alone art our Almighty One.
Give us wisdom without guile,
Establish us and strengthen us,
Thou Everlasting One.

SWEDEN

Words by
RICHARD DYBECK (1811-1877)

Composer unknown
Arr. EDVIN KALLSTENIUS

First sung in 1844 with the title 'Sång till Norden' (Song to the North);
Its use as a National Anthem dates from 1880-1890.

sol, din him - mel, di - na äng - der grö - na, Din
sun, thy skies, thy verd - ant mead - ows smil - ing, Thy

sol din him - mel, di - na äng - der grö - na.
sun, thy skies, thy verd - ant mead - ows smil - ing.

2. *Du tronar på minnen från fornstora dar,*
   Då ärat ditt namn flög över jorden.
   Jag vet, att du är och du blir vad du var,
   Ack, jag vill leva, jag vill dö i Norden! *(repeat)*

Translation

2. Thy throne rests on mem'ries from great days of yore,
   When world-wide renown was valour's guerdon.
   I know to thy name thou art true as before.
   Oh, I would live and I would die in Sweden. *(repeat)*

SWITZERLAND
Swiss Psalm

Words*
(German) by LEONHARD WIDMER (1808-1868)
(French) by Ch. CHATELANET
(Surselvisch) by J. A. BÜHLER

Music by
ALBERICH ZWYSSIG (1808-1854)
Arr. by OTTO KREIS

The original version dates from 1841. Adopted by the Federal Government as the official National Anthem in 1961. This officially approved arrangement published by Krompholz and Co., Berne.

*The authors of the Italian, Ladinisch and English versions are unknown.

Eu - re from-me / See - le ahnt, / Eu - re from-me / See - le ahnt / Gott / im heh -ren
Au ciel mon-tent / plus joy-eux, / Au ciel mon-tent / plus joy-eux / Les / ac - cents d'un
In fa - vor del / pa - trio suol, / In fa - vor del / pa - trio suol, / Cit - / ta - di-no Id-
Leu eis Ti cun / cor pa-tern, / Leu eis Ti cun / cor pa-tern, / O / al - tis - sim
Ti - a or - ma / sain - ta ferm, / Ti - a or - ma / sain - ta ferm, / Dieu / in tschêl, il
For you feel and / un - der-stand, / For you feel and / un - der-stand / That / He dwell -eth

Va - ter - land, ___ / Gott, / den Herrn, im / heh - ren / Va - ter - land!
cœur pi - eux, ___ / Les / ac - cents é - mus / d'un / cœur ___ pi - eux.
dio lo vuol, ___ / Cit - / ta - di - no Dio, / si / Dio ___ lo vuol.
Bab e - tern! ___ / O / al - tis - sim Bab, / o / Bab ___ e - tern!
bap e - tern! ___ / Dieu / in tschêl · il bap, / il / bap ___ e - tern!
in this land, ___ / That / He dwell - eth / in ___ this land.

GERMAN

2. Kommst im Abendglühn daher,
   Find' ich dich im Sternenheer,
   Dich, du Menschenfreundlicher, Liebender!
   In des Himmels lichten Räumen
   Kann ich froh und selig träumen;
   Denn die fromme Seele ahnt (twice)
   Gott im hehren Vaterland!
   Gott, den Herrn, im hehren Vaterland!

3. Ziehst im Nebelflor daher,
   Such' ich dich im Wolkenmeer,
   Dich, du Unergründlicher, Ewiger!
   Aus dem grauen Luftgebilde
   Bricht die Sonne klar und milde,
   Und die fromme Seele ahnt (twice)
   Gott im hehren Vaterland!
   Gott, den Herrn, im hehren Vaterland!

4. Fahrst im wilden Sturm daher,
   Bist du selbst uns Hort und Wehr,
   Du, allmächtig Waltender, Rettender!
   In Gewitternacht und Grauen
   Lasst uns kindlich ihm vertrauen!
   Ja, die fromme Seele ahnt (twice)
   Gott im hehren Vaterland,
   Gott, den Herrn, im hehren Vaterland.

FRENCH

2. Lorsqu'un doux rayon du soir
   Joue encore dans le bois noir,
   Le cœur se sent plus heureux près de Dieu.
   Loin des vains bruits de la plaine
   L'âme en paix est plus sereine;
   Au ciel montent plus joyeux (twice)
   Les accents d'un cœur pieux,
   Les accents émus d'un cœur pieux.

3. Lorsque dans la sombre nuit
   La foudre éclate avec bruit,
   Notre cœur pressent encore le Dieu fort;
   Dans l'orage et la détresse,
   Il est notre forteresse.
   Offrons-lui des cœurs pieux, (twice)
   Dieu nous bénira des cieux,
   Dieu nous bénira du haut des cieux.

4. Des grands monts vient le secours,
   Suisse, espère en Dieu toujours!
   Garde la foi des aïeux, vis comme eux!
   Sur l'autel de la patrie
   Mets tes biens, ton cœur, ta vie!
   C'est le trésor précieux (twice)
   Que Dieu bénira des cieux,
   Que Dieu bénira du haut des cieux.

ITALIAN

2. Se di nubi un velo
   M'asconde il tuo cielo,
   Pel tuo raggio anelo,
   Dio d'amor.
   Fuga o sole quei vapori
   E mi rendi i tuoi favori
   Di mia patria deh, pietà! (twice)
   Brilla, o sol di verità,
   Brilla sol, o sol di verità!

SURSELVISCH *

2. Cu'l sulegl, ch'ha tut sclariu
   Va la sera da rendiu:
   Ves jeu tei tras la splendur
   Donatur!
   Contas steilas tarlischontas
   Van sur mei, salid purtontas:
   Leu eis Ti cun cor patern, (twice)
   O Altissim! Bab etern!
   O altissim Bab, o Bab etern!

3. Cu'l sulegl ei stgirentaus
   Da snavur il cor curclaus
   Sent jeu tei, Empaladur
   Dil futur!
   Tras las neblas penetrescha
   Glisch, che mund e cor sclarescha:
   Leu eis Ti cun cor patern, (twice)
   O Altissim! Bab etern!
   O altissim Bab, o Bab etern!

4. Cu la furia digl orcan
   Fa tremblar il cor human:
   Dattas i a nus vigur,
   O Signur!
   Els orcans ils pli sgarscheivels,
   Stein nus sco nos cuolms stateivels:
   Leu eis Ti cun cor patern, (twice)
   O Altissim! Bab etern!
   O altissim Bab, o Bab etern!

*Rhaeto-Romansh of the Rhine valleys.

LADINISCH*

2. Eir la saira in splendur
    Da las stailas in l'azur
    Tai chattain nus, creatur,
    Tuot pussant!
    Cur cha'l firmamaint sclarescha
    In noss cours fidanza crescha.
    Tia orma sainta ferm, (twice)
    Dieu in tschêl, il bap etern!
    Dieu in tschêl, il bap, il bap etern!

Tü a nus nun est zoppà
Cur il tschêl in nüvlas sta,
Tü imperscrutabel spiert,
Tuot pussant!
Tschêl e terra t'obedeschan,
Vents e nüvlas secundeschan.
Tia orma sainta ferm, (twice)
Dieu in tschêl, il bap etern!
Dieu in tschêl, il bap, il bap etern!

4. Eir l'orcan plü furius
    Nun at muossa main a nus,
    Sco il dirigent dal muond,
    Tuot pussant!
    Eir in temporals terribels
    Sun teis uordens bain visibels.
    Tia orma sainta ferm, (twice)
    Dieu in tschêl, il bap etern!
    Dieu in tschêl, il bap, il bap etern!

Rhaeto-Romansh of Engadine.

ENGLISH

2. In the sunset Thou art nigh
    And beyond the starry sky,
    Thou, O loving Father, ever near.
    When to Heav'n we are departing,
    Joy and bliss Thou'lt be imparting,
    For we feel and understand (twice)
    That Thou dwellest in this land. (twice)

3. When dark clouds enshroud the hills
    And grey mist the valley fills,
    Yet Thou art not hidden from Thy sons.
    Pierce the gloom in which we cower
    With Thy sunshine's cleansing power;
    Then we'll feel and understand (twice)
    That God dwelleth in this land. (twice)

SYRIA

Words by
KHALIL MARDAM BEY (1895-1959)

Music by
MUHAMMAD SALIM FLAYFEL (*b.* 1899) an
AHMAD SALIM FLAYFEL (*b.* 1906)

Officially adopted in 1936.

Ru - bu - 'u Al-sha-a - mi Bur - u - ju Al-'al - ai Tu - ha - ki Sa - ma - a

Bi - 'a - li Al-sa - nai Fa - ar - dhun Za - hat

Bil - shum-usa Al-wid - hai Sa - ma - un La'am-ri - ka Aw Kal - sa-ma.

Translation

Defenders of the realm,
Peace on you;
Our proud spirits will
Not be subdued.
The abode of Arabism,
A hallowed sanctuary;
The seat of the stars,
An inviolable preserve.

Syria's plains are
Towers in the heights,
Resembling the sky
Above the clouds.
A land resplendent
With brilliant suns,
Becoming another sky,
Or almost a sky.

TAIWAN
Republic of China

Words based on a speech by
Dr. SUN YAT-SEN (1866-1925)
Translation by
TU T'ING-HSIU

Music by
CHENG MAO-YUN (b. 1900
Arr. by Prof. HUANG CHIH

Maestoso

San min chu I, wo tang so
"San min chu I," our aim shall

chung, I kien min kuo, I chin - ta
be, To found a free land, world peace be our

tung. Tze erh to shih, wei min chien feng, su
stand. Lead on com-rades, van-guards ye are, Hold

Adopted as the National Anthem in 1929.
The words 'San Min Chu I' express Dr. Sun's political philosophy of the Three People's Principles,
i.e. government of the people, by the people, and for the people.
* Year of death unknown.

yeh fei shieh, chu I shih tsung, shih ching shih
fast your aim, by sun and star, Be earn - est and

yung, pi shing pi chung, I
brave, your coun - try to save, One

hsin I teh, kuan cheh shih chung!
heart, one soul, one mind one goal!

TANZANIA

Words written collectively

Music by
MANKAYI ENOCH SONTONGA* (d. 1904)†
Arr. by V.E. WEBSTER

Moderato

1. Mun-gu i-ba-ri-ki A - fri - ca
2. Mun-gu i-ba-ri-ki Tan-gan-yi-ka

Wa-ba-ri-ki Vion-go-zi wa-ke He-ki-ma U-mo-ja na
Du-mi-sha u-hu-ru na Umo-ja Wa-ke kwa Wa-u-me na

A - ma - ni Hi - zi ni ngao ze - tu
Wa - to - to Mun - gu I - ba - ri - ki

* By permission of Lovedale Press, Cape Province, South Africa.

The words of this anthem are composed from the six prize-winning entries to the competition announced by the Minister of Education on 31 July, 1961. It became the National Anthem when Tanganyika achieved independence on 9 December, 1961 and was retained as a National Anthem when Tanzania was formed by the union of Tanganyika and Zanzibar on 26 April, 1964.

The music is a shorter version of N'kosi Sikelel'i Africa (see the National Anthems of Zambia and Zimbabwe).

† Year of birth unknown.

CHORUS

Afrika na watu wake. Ibariki
Tanzania na watu wake. Ibariki

Afrika Ibariki Afrika
Tanzania Ibariki Tanzania

Tubariki watoto wa Afrika.
Tubariki watoto wa Tanzania.

Official Translation

1. God Bless Africa.
   Bless its leaders.
   Let Wisdom Unity and
   Peace be the shield of
   Africa and its people.

   CHORUS Bless Africa,
   Bless Africa,
   Bless the children of Africa.

2. God Bless Tanzania.
   Grant eternal Freedom and Unity
   to its sons and daughters.
   God Bless Tanganyika and its People.

   CHORUS Bless Tanzania,
   Bless Tanzania,
   Bless the children of Tanzania.

THAILAND
Phleng Chat

Words by
Col. LUANGSARANUPRAPAN (1896-1954)

Music by
Prof. PRACHENDURIYANG (1883-1968)

Pra thet___ thai ru - am nu ' a chat chu'a thai___ Pen pra

cha rat___ pha thai kho'ng thai thuk suan___ Yu dam rong khong wai___dai thang

muan Duay thai lu - an mai___ rak sa mak khi Thai ni

Adopted in 1939.

rak sa ngop   tae thu'ng rop mai khalt   Ek ka   rat čha mai hai khrai khom khi   Sa la___

luat thuk yat___pen chat   phli   Tha loeng pra thet chat thai tha wi   mi chai chai   yo.

Translation

Thailand, cradle of Thais wherever they may be,
The homeland of our people,
The whole land is the land of the Thais.
United and in the spirit of brotherhood
We are ever able to defend our land.
Thais love peace, but never fear the battle.
Never shall we let our independence be surrendered.
We will shed every drop of our blood
To defend our beloved country.
May glory and victory reign over our beloved Kingdom.

TOGO

Words and music written collectively by the
RASSEMBLEMENT DU PEUPLE TOGOLAIS
Arr. W.L. REED

This replaced the former anthem in 1979.

li - sme.___ Les rè - gle -ments de compte, la haine et l'a - nar - chie Ne font que frei - ner___ la ré - vo - lu -tion. Si nous sommes di - vi - sés,_____ l'en -ne -mi s'in - fil - tre___ Dans nos rangs pour nous ex - ploi-

2. *N'oublions pas du tout l'appel historique du 30 Août 1969.*
   Ecoutons-le retentir à jamais.
   Notre voie de salut c'est le Rassemblement.
   Rassemblement de tous les Togolais
   Pour la grande victoire. Togolais debout!
   Portons haut le flambeau de l'Union.

   CHORUS *A l'Union etc.*

3. *Ecartons le mauvais esprit qui gêne l'Unité Africaine.*
   Ecartons-le tout comme l'Impérialisme.
   Les coups de canons et les coups de fusils
   Ne font que freiner l'élan de l'Afrique.
   De notre désunion l'Impérialisme profite,
   Profite bien pour nous opposer.

   CHORUS *La paix - la paix - la paix -*
   Oh, Dieu! la paix -
   La paix pour l'Afrique!

Translation by T.M. Cartledge

1. Let us put aside every bad feeling
   That hinders national unity.
   Let us fight such feelings as we fought imperialism.
   Settling accounts with people, hatred and anarchy
   Only serve to hold back the revolution.
   If we are divided, the enemy infiltrates
   Our ranks to exploit us.

   CHORUS Togolese! Our ancestors are calling us to unity.
   Peace, peace, peace, oh Togolese,
   Is what our forefathers demand of us.

2. Let us never forget the historic appeal
   Of August 30th 1969.
   Our way to well-being is the massing,
   The massing of all Togolese
   For the great victory. Arise, Togolese!
   Let us carry high the torch of unity.

   CHORUS Togolese! etc.

3. Let us put aside the bad feelings
   That hinder African unity.
   The firing of cannons and rifles
   Only holds back Africa's impetus.
   Imperialism takes advantage of our disunity,
   Takes great advantage of it for opposing us.

   CHORUS Peace, peace, peace, oh God!
   Peace, peace for Africa!

TONGA

Words by
Prince UELINGATONI NGU TUPOUMALOHI
(1854-1885)

Music by
KARL GUSTAVUS SCHMITT
(1834-1900)

'E 'O-tu-a Ma-fi-ma-fi, Ko ho mau 'Ei - ki Ko- e,
Oh, Al-migh-ty God a-bove, Thou art our Lord and sure de-fence,

Ko Koe Koe fa la-la 'a-nga, Mo ia 'o-fa ki To- nga;
In our good-ness we do trust Thee And our To-nga Thou dost love;

'A - fio hi-fo 'e-mau lo-tu, 'A ia 'o-ku mau fai ni,
Hear our prayer, for though un-seen we know that Thou hast blessed our land;

Mo Ke ta-li ho-mau lo-to, 'O ma-la-'i 'a Tu-pou.
Grant our earn-est sup-pli-ca-tion, Guard and save Tu-pou our King.

The first reported singing of this anthem dates from July 1874,
but it was probably in use earlier.

TRINIDAD and TOBAGO

Words and music by
PATRICK STANISLAUS CASTAGNE (*b.* 1916)

li - ber - ty, in the fires of hope and prayer, With bound-less faith in our des - ti - ny, we so-lemn - ly de - clare:

The National Anthem officially came into use at midnight on 31 August, 1962 at the Flag Raising Ceremony held outside Parliament Buildings, Port of Spain. It was chosen as the result of a competition held by the Government.

434

TUNISIA

Words by
JALALEDDINE EL-NACCACHE (*b.* 1910)
English translation by
ISMAIL HASSAN
Versification by
T.M. CARTLEDGE

Music by
SALAH MEHDI (*b.* 1925)
Arr. by T.M. CARTLEDGE

Tempo di Marcia

f CHORUS

A - la Khal - li - di Ya Di - ma - nal - gha - wa - li Dji -
Im - mor - tal and pre - cious the blood we— have shed for our

ha - dal - wa - tan Li - tah - ri - ri Khad - ra - 'i -
dear fath - er - land. In or - der to free our green

na La - nu Ba - li Bi Ak - sal Mi - han Dji -
land a - ny hard - ship we glad - ly will stand. The

Officially adopted 20 March, 1958.

ha - dun Ta - hal - la Bi Nas - rim - mu - bin 'Al - al Gha - si - bin 'Al-
fight is made sweet by a vic - to - ry sure Re - mov - ing the yoke we've

al Ha - ki - min Tu - ghat Iz - za - man Na -
had to en - dure. The fire we con - front as

- khu - dul - la - Hib Bi Ru - hil Ha - bib Za - 'im Il - wa - tan
faith - ful we keep The spi - rit of our great lead - er Ha - bib.

Fine

437

da' - al U - khuw - wa - ti Wal - it - ti - had Wa
true broth - er - hood and to true u - ni - ty. Be

Thu - dul - 'i - da 'An - hi - ma Ar - di - na Wa
rea - dy, like li - ons pre - pared for the fight, De-

Ku - nu U - su - dan Bi - yaw - mil Dji - lad. A-
-fend - ing our coun - try from each en - e - my. Im-

CHORUS

2. *Warithnal-jilada Wa Majdan-nidal*
   Wa Fi Ardina Masra 'Ul-ghasibin.
   Wa Salat Asatilina Fin-nizal
   Tamuju Bi 'Abtalinal-fatihin.
   Liwa 'Ul-Kifahi Bihathash-shimal
   Rafa-'nahu Yawmal-fida Bil-yamin.

   CHORUS

3. *Shababal-'ola 'Izzuna Bil-hima*
   Wa 'Izzul-hima Bish-shababil-'atid.
   Lina Himmatun Talatil-'anjuma
   Tu 'Idul-ma 'Ali Wa Tabnil-jadid.
   Fahayyul-liwa Khafiqan Fis-sama
   Bi 'Izzin Wa Fakhrin Wa Nasrin Majid.

   CHORUS

2. The glory and fight we inherit today.
   Oppressors were fought here on this battleground.
   Our legions in fury attacked in the field
   As heroes in waves let their war-cries resound.
   The banner of war in the North we have raised,
   By oath we to ransom our land all are bound.

   CHORUS

3. O noble the youth, our defence you assure,
   Defending our honour, as ready you be.
   Our strong aspirations reach up to the sky
   That greatness return and a new day we see.
   The flag, as it waves in the sky, now salute
   With honour and glory and great victory.

   CHORUS

TURKEY
Istıklâl Marsi
(The March of Independence)

Words by
MEHMET AKIF ERSOY (1873-1936)
English versification by
T.M. CARTLEDGE

Music by
ZEKİ ÜNGÖR (1880-1958)
Arr. by T.M. CARTLEDGE

* Lower notes optional for bass or alto voices.

Officially adopted on 12 March, 1921.

2. Çatma kurban olayım çehreni ey nazlı hilâl
   Kahraman ırkıma bir gül ne bu şiddet bu celâl
   Sana olmaz dökülen kanlarımız sonra helâl
   Hakkıdır hakka tapan milletimin istiklâl.

2. Frown not, fair crescent, for I
   Am ready e'en to die for thee.
   Smile now upon my heroic nation, leave this anger,
        lest the blood shed for thee unblessed be.
   Freedom's the right of this my nation,
   Yes, freedom for us who worship God and seek what's right.

TUVALU

Words and music by
AFAESE MANOA (*b.* 1942

First sung on Independence Day, 1 October, 1978, when it was officially adopted.

a - mō__ fa - ka - ta - si A - te a - tu fe - nu - a._____ "Tu -
build on a sure foun - da - tion When we trust in God's great law;_____ "Tu -

va - lu mo te A - tu - a" Ki te se ga - ta ma - i!
va - lu for The Al - migh - ty" Be our song for e - ver - more!

Translation by J. F. Wilson

2. Tuku atu tau pulega
   Ki te pule mai luga,
   Kilo tonu ki ou mua
   Me ko ia e tautai.
   "Pule tasi mo ia"
   Ki te se gata mai,
   Ko tena mana
   Ko tou malosi tena.
   Pati lima kae kalaga
   Ulufonu ki te tupu.
   "Tuvalu ko tu saoloto"
   Ki te se gata mai.

2. Let our trust our lives henceforward
   To the King to whom we pray,
   With our eyes fixed firmly on Him
   He is showing us the way.
   "May we reign with Him in glory"
   Be our song for evermore,
   For His almighty power
   Is our strength from shore to shore.
   Shout aloud in jubilation
   To the King Whom we adore.
   "Tuvalu free and united"
   Be our song for evermore!

UGANDA

Words and music by
GEORGE WILBERFORCE KAKOMA (*b.* 1923)

With Dignity

1. Oh U - gan - da! may God up - hold thee, We lay our fu-ture in thy hand. U - ni - ted,free, For lib - er - ty To - geth - er we'll al - ways stand.

2. Oh Uganda! the land of freedom,
    Our love and labour we give,
    And with neighbours all
    At our country's call
    In peace and friendship we'll live.

3. Oh Uganda! the land that feeds us
    By sun and fertile soil grown,
    For our own dear land
    We'll always stand,
    The Pearl of Africa's Crown.

This National Anthem was selected through a competition, and came into use when the country became independent on 9 October, 1962.

UNION OF SOVIET SOCIALIST REPUBLICS

Words by
SERGEI VLADIMIROVICH MIKHALKOV (*b.*1913) and
GAROLD GABRIELEVICH EL-REGISTAN (*b.*1924)*

Music by
ALEKSANDR VASILIEVICH ALEKSANDROV
(1883-1946)

This became officially the Soviet National Anthem in 1943, replacing the "International".
*Words were slightly changed in 1977.

di - ni mo - gu - chi So - vyet - ski So - yuz!

CHORUS

Sláv - sya,___ O - tye - chest - vo

na - she___ svo - bod - no - ye,

Druzh - bi na - ro - dov na - dyozh - ni op - lot! ___ Par - ti - a ___

Le - ni - na, si - la ___ na - rod - nya - ya

Nas k tor - zhe - stvu Kom - mu - niz - ma vi - dyot! 2. Skvoz

1 & 2.

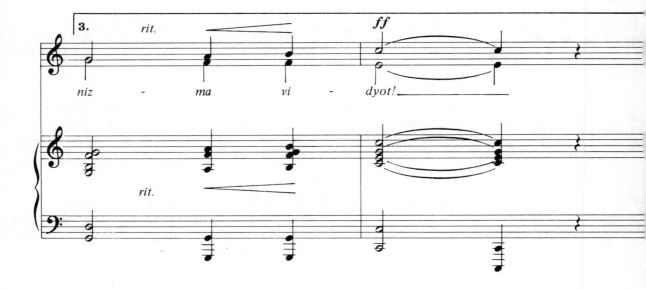

niz - ma vi - dyot!

2. *Skvoz' grozi siyalo nam solntse svobodi,*
   I Lenin veliki nam put' ozaril:
   Na pravoye delo on podnyal narodi,
   Na trud i na podvigi nas vdokhnovil!

3. *V pobyedye bessmyertnykh idey Kommunizma*
   Mi vidim gryadushchie nashey strani,
   I krasnomu znamyeni slavnoi Otchizni
   Mi budyem vsegda bezzavyetno verni!

Translation by Herbert Marshall and Sophie V. Satin

1. Unbreakable Union of free-born Republics
   Great Russia has welded for ever to stand.
   Thy might was created by will of our peoples,
   Now flourish in unity, great Soviet Land!

CHORUS Sing to our Motherland, home of the free,
   Bulwark of peoples in brotherhood strong!
   The Party of Lenin, the strength of our peoples,
   To Communism's triumph lead us on!

2. Through tempests the sunrays of freedom have cheered us
   Along the new path where great Lenin did lead.
   To a righteous cause he raised up the peoples,
   Inspired them to labour and heroic deeds.

CHORUS

3. In the victory of Communism's deathless ideals
   We see the future of our dear Land,
   And to her fluttering scarlet banner
   Selflessly true we always shall stand!

CHORUS

UNITED ARAB EMIRATES

Music by
MOHAMED ABDEL WAHAB (*b.* 1915)
Arranged from the band score by
W.L. REED

o words

Officially adopted in 1971.

UNITED STATES OF AMERICA
The Star-Spangled Banner

Words by
FRANCIS SCOTT KEY (1779-1843)

Composer unknown*

1. O — say! can you see, by the dawn's ear - ly
stripes and bright stars, thro' the pe - ril - ous

light, What so proud - ly we hail'd at the
fight, O'er the ram - parts we watch'd were so

twi - light's last gleam - ing, Whose broad
gal - lant - ly stream - ing? And the

Words and music officially designated as the National Anthem by Act of Congress approved by the President
March, 1931.

By permission of J.B. Cramer & Co. Ltd.

* The English composer John Stafford Smith (c. 1750-1836) in his fifth collection of glees (1799) published
an arrangement of 'To Anacreon in Heaven', the tune to which Francis Scott Key later wrote 'The Star-Spangled
Banner'. This has led to his being mistakenly regarded as the composer of the tune, whose actual origin is
unknown.

land ___ of the free and the home of the brave?

2. On the shore, dimly seen thro' the mists of the deep,
Where the foe's haughty host in dread silence reposes,
What is that which the breeze, o'er the towering steep,
As it fitfully blows, half conceals, half discloses?
Now it catches the gleam of the morning's first beam,
In full glory reflected now shines on the stream;
'Tis the Star-Spangled Banner, O long may it wave
O'er the land of the free and the home of the brave.

3. O thus be it ever when free man shall stand
Between their loved homes and the war's desolation!
Blest with vict'ry and peace, may the heav'n-rescued land
Praise the Pow'r that hath made and preserved us a nation.
Then conquer we must, for our cause it is just,
And this be our motto: "In God is our trust".
And the Star-Spangled Banner in triumph shall wave
O'er the land of the free and the home of the brave.

URUGUAY

454

Words by
FRANCISCO ESTEBAN ACUÑA de FIGUEROA
(1791-1862)
English versification by
T.M. CARTLEDGE

Music by
FRANCISCO JOSÉ DEBALI (1791-1859)*
Arr. by G. GRASSO

Reproduced by permission of Recordi Americana S.A.E.C. Buenos Aires.
Officially adopted as the National Anthem by a government decree of 18 July, 1845.
The author also wrote the words for the National Anthem of Paraguay.
* Francisco Debali also composed the music for the National Anthem of Paraguay.

sa - bre - mos cum - plir,
ful - fil, cour - age high,

sa - bre - mos cum -
ful - fil, cour - age

- plir, sa - bre - mos cum - plir.
high, ful - fil, cour - age high.

Fine

Moderato

p **VERSE**

¡Li - ber - tad,! ¡li - ber - tad,! O - rien - ta — les Es - te
Li - ber - ty, Li - ber - ty, East - ern lands — men! 'Twas this

p

grí - to_a la Pa - tria sal - vó! Que_a sus bra - vos en fie - ras ba -
cry saved our coun - try of yore, And in - flam - ing its he - roes with

mf   *p*

dal ℀ al Fine

DD

VANUATU

Words and music by
FRANÇOIS VINCENT (*b.* 1955)
Arr. by W.L. REED

Allegro moderato

Yu - mi, Yu - mi, Yu - mi i glat blong

ta - lem se, Yu - mi, Yu - mi, Yu - mi i man blong

Va - nu - a - tu! 2. Plan - te fa - sin blong bi - fo___ i stap, Plan - te
1. God i giv - im ples ia long___ yu - mi, Yu - mi
3. Yu - mi sa - ve plan - te wok___ i stap, Long ol

Adopted in 1980

mi   i glat blong ta - lem se,   Yu - mi,   Yu -

mi,   Yu - mi   i   man blong Va - nu - a - tu!

rall . . . .

Translation by Parai K. Tamei

We are happy to proclaim
We are the People of Vanuatu!

1. God has given us this land;
   This gives us great cause for rejoicing.
   We are strong, we are free in this land;
   We are all brothers.

We are happy to proclaim
We are the People of Vanuatu!

2. We have many traditions
   And we are finding new ways.
   Now we shall be one People,
   We shall be united for ever.

We are happy to proclaim
We are the People of Vanuatu!

3. We know there is much work to be done
   On all our islands.
   May God, our Father, help us!

We are happy to proclaim
We are the People of Vanuatu!

VATICAN CITY STATE
Inno and Marcia Pontificale

Words by
ANTONIO ALLEGRA (1905-1969)

Music by
CHARLES GOUNOD (1818-1893)

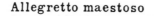

Allegretto maestoso

Inno (Hymn)

This became the official hymn in 1950. It is played (1) In the presence of the Holy Father. (2) In the presence of one of his Special Legates. (3) On the occasion of the presentation of Credential Letters by a Nuncio of the Holy See.

The music is reproduced by permission of Institut fur Auslandsbeziehungen, Stuttgart, and taken from *Die National-Hymnen Der Erde*.

gno - re,___ Pa - ce ai_ Fe-de - li, di Cri - sto nel - l'a -

mo - re. A____ Te ve-nia - mo, An - ge - li - co Pa -

mf

p   *cresc.*

sto - re, In____ Te ve-dia - mo il mi - te Re - den -

dim. *p*   *cresc.*

to - re, E - - - re-de San - to di ve - ra e san - ta

f *dim.* *p*   *cresc.*

Marcia Pontificale (Pontifical March)

Ro - ma lu - ce del - le gen - - ti, il mon_do spe - ra in

te! Sal - ve Sal - ve Ro - ma, la tua

lu - ce non tra - mon - ta, Vin - ce l'o - dio e

l'on - ta lo splen-dor di__ tua bel - tà._____

Ro - ma de-gli A-po - sto - li   Ma-dre e gui-da dei Re - den - ti,

Ro-ma lu-ce del-le gen - ti,   il   mon-do spe - ra in te!

Translation
PONTIFICAL HYMN

O Rome immortal, city of martyrs and saints,
O immortal Rome, accept our praises.
Glory in the heavens to God our Lord
And peace to men who love Christ!

To you we come, angelic Pastor,
In you we see the gentle Redeemer.
You are the holy heir of our Faith,
You are the comfort and the refuge of those who believe and fight.

Force and terror will not prevail,
But truth and love will reign.

PONTIFICAL MARCH

Hail, O Rome,
Eternal abode of memories;
A thousand palms and a thousand altars
Sing your praises.

O city of the Apostles,
Mother and guide of the elect,
Light of the nations,
And hope of the world!

Hail, O Rome!
Your light will never fade;
The splendour of your beauty
Disperses hatred and shame.

O city of the Apostles
Mother and guide of the elect,
Light of the nations,
And hope of the world!

VENEZUELA

Words by
VINCENTE SALIAS (1786-1816)
English versification by
T.M. CARTLEDGE

Music by
JUAN JOSÉ LANDAETA (1780-1814)
Arr. by HENRY COLEMAN

Adopted as National Anthem 25 May, 1881, by a government decree.

a tempo
cresc.

el vil e - go - is - mo que otra vez triun - fó.
The foul self - ish ty - rant Who once tri - umphed here.

2. *Gritemos con brío:*
    Muera la opresión!
    Compatriotas fieles
    la fuerza es la unión:
    y desde el Empíreo
    el Supremo Autor
    un sublime aliento
    al pueblo infundió.

    CORO

3. *Unida con lazos*
    que el cielo formó,
    la América toda
    existe en Nación;
    y si el despotismo
    levanta la voz
    seguid el ejemplo
    que Caracas dió.

    CORO

2. Let's cry out aloud:
    May oppression banished be!
    Faithful countrymen, your strength
    Lives in your unity.
    And from highest heaven
    The great Creater breathed;
    A spirit sublime
    Among us here bequeathed.

    CHORUS

3. United by bonds
    Made by heav'n's creative hand,
    All America exists
    As one united land.
    And if tyranny
    Should dare to raise its head,
    Let all of us follow
    Where Caracas has led.

    CHORUS

VIETNAM

Words and music by
VAN CAO (b. 1923)

Adopted as national anthem by the Provisional Government of the Democratic Republic of Vietnam from the first days of its formation, and by the National Assembly in its second session in November 1946.
In July 1976 the first election of the United National Assembly adopted this national anthem for the whole country.

quang xây xác quân thù Thăng gian lao, cùng nhau lập chiến
lâu ta nuốt căm hờn Quyết hy sinh, đời ta tươi thắm

khu. Vì nhân dân chiến đấu không ngừng Tiến mau
hơn. Vì nhân dân chiến đấu không ngừng Tiến mau

ra sa trường. Tiến lên!_____ Cùng tiến
ra sa trường. Tiến lên!_____ Cùng tiến

lên!_____ Nước non Việt-nam ta vững bền.
lên!_____ Nước non Việt-nam ta vững

1.
2. Đoàn quân Việt-
2.
bền.

8....

French Translation

1. *Soldats vietnamiens, nous allons de l'avant,*
   Mus par une même volonté de sauver la patrie.
   Nos pas redoublés sonnent sur la route longue et rude.
   Notre drapeau, rouge du sang de la victoire, porte l'âme de la nation.
   Le lointain grondement des canons rythme les accents de notre marche.
   Le chemin de la gloire se pave de cadavres ennemis.
   Triomphant des difficultés, ensemble, nous édifions nos bases de résistance.
   Jurons de lutter sans répit pour la cause du peuple.
   Courons vers le champ de bataille!
   En avant! Tous ensemble, en avant!
   Notre patrie vietnamienne est solide et durable.

2. *Soldats vietamiens, nous allons de l'avant,*
   L'etoile d'or au vent
   Conduisant notre peuple et notre patrie hors de la misère et des souffrances.
   Unissons nos efforts dans la lutte pour l'édification de la vie nouvelle.
   Debout! d'un même élan, rompons nos fers!
   Depuis si longtemps, nous avons contenu notre haine!
   Soyons prêts à tous les sacrifices et notre vie sera radieuse.
   Jurons de lutter sans répit pour la cause du peuple,
   Courons vers le champ de bataille!
   En avant! Tous ensemble, en avant!
   Notre patrie vietnamienne est solide et durable.

English Translation

1. Soldiers of Vietnam, we go forward,
   With the one will to save our Fatherland,
   Our hurried steps are sounding on the long and arduous road.
   Our flag, red with the blood of victory, bears the spirit
     of our country.
   The distant rumbling of the guns mingles with our marching song.
   The path to glory passes over the bodies of our foes.
   Overcoming all hardships, together we build our resistance bases.
   Ceaselessly for the people's cause we struggle,
   Hastening to the battle-field!
   Forward! All together advancing!
   Our Vietnam is strong, eternal.

2. Soldiers of Vietnam, we go forward!
   The gold star of our flag in the wind
   Leading our people, our native land, out of misery and suffering.
   Let us join our efforts in the fight for the building of a new life.
   Let us stand up and break our chains.
   For too long have we swallowed our hatred.
   Let us keep ready for all sacrifices and our life will be radiant.
   Ceaselessly for the people's cause we struggle,
   Hastening to the battle-field!
   Forward! All together advancing!
   Our Vietnam is strong, eternal.

WALES
Hen Wlad fy Nhadau
(Land of my Fathers)

Words by
EVAN JAMES (1809-1893)
English translation by
W.S. GWYNN WILLIAMS

Music by
JAMES JAMES (1833-1902)
Arr. by W.S. GWYNN WILLIAM

1. Mae hen wlad fy nhad-au yn an nwyl i mi, Gwlad beirdd a chan-tor-ion, en-wog-ion o fri; Ei gwr-ol ry-fel-wyr, gwlad-gar-wyr tra mâd, Tros rydd-id coll-as-ant eu gwaed. Gwlad, gwlad,

1. The land of my fath-ers is dear un-to me, Old land where the min-strels are hon-oured and free; Its war-ring de-fen-ders so gal-lant and brave, For free-dom their life's blood they gave. Home, home,

This national song was first sung at the famous Llangollen Eisteddfod of 1858, and is now regarded as having the status of a National Anthem. It is also sung as an anthem in Brittany, to a Breton version by J. Taldir.

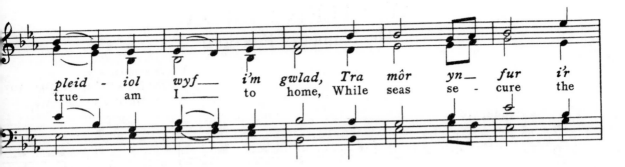

pleid - iol wyf___ i'm gwlad, Tra môr yn__ fur i'r
true___ am I___ to home, While seas se - cure the

bur hoff bau, O bydd - ed i'r hen-iaith bar - hau.
land so__ pure, O may the old lan-guage en - dure.

2. *Hen Gymru fynyddig, paradwys y bardd,*
    Pob dyffryn, pob clogwyn i'm golwg sydd hardd;
    Trwy deimlad gwladgarol, mor swynol yw si
    Ei nentydd, afonydd, i mi.

    Gwlad, gwlad, etc.

3. *Os treisiodd y gelyn fy ngwlad tan ei droed,*
    Mae hen iaith y Cymry mor fyw ag erioed;
    Ni luddiwyd yr awen gan erchyll law brad,
    Na thelyn berseiniol fy ngwlad.

    Gwlad, gwlad, etc.

2. Old land of the mountains, the Eden of bards,
    Each gorge and each valley a loveliness guards;
    Through love of my country, charmed voices will be
    Its streams, and its rivers, to me.

    Home, home, etc.

3. Though foemen have trampled my land 'neath their feet,
    The language of Cambria still knows no retreat;
    The muse is not vanquished by traitor's fell hand,
    Nor silenced the harp of my land.

    Home, home, etc.

WESTERN SAMOA
The Banner of Freedom

Words and music by
SAUNI IIGA KURESA (1900-197
Arr. by HENRY COLEMAN

Copyright, 1948, by Sauni Iiga Kuresa.
On 1 January, 1962, Western Samoa became the first sovereign independent Polynesian State. This anthem wa
selected by the Council of the Committee to be the National Anthem and sung as the flag of the Wester
Samoan Government was raised.

fe - fe, o le Atua lo ta fa'a vae — O lo - ta

Sa'o lo - to - ga, Sa - moa, tu - la'i, ia

a - gia - gia lau Fu'a lou pa - le le - a.

Translation

Samoa, arise and raise your banner that is your crown!

Oh! see and behold the stars on the waving banner!
They are a sign that Samoa is able to lead.

Oh! Samoa, hold fast
Your freedom for ever!

Do not be afraid; as you are founded on God;
Our treasured precious liberty.
Samoa, arise and wave
Your banner that is your crown!

YEMEN
Arab Republic

Words by
AHMED AL-AMARI (*b.* 1922)

Music by
ALI BIN ALI AL-ANESI (1933-1981)
Arr. by W.L. REED

Adopted in 1978

Tempo I°

ff

Fi Zilli Rayati Thawrati
       A Lantu Jumhuriyati
Yamani S-sa Idatu Munyati
       Inni Wahabtuka Muhjati
Bi-azimati Bi-iradati
       Anhaytu Ahada Z-zulmati
Wa-bi-quwati Wa-bi-wahdati
       Haqqaqtu Huluma L-ummati
Wa-madaytu Nahwa L-qimmati
       Wa-allahu Baraka Wathbati
Hayhata Sha Bi Yastakin
       Sha Bi Maha Zulma S-sinin
Wa-abada Kulla Z-zalimin
       Li-ya Isha Marfu A L-jabin

Translation

Under the shade of the Banner of the Revolution
We proclaimed our Republic;

The Happy Yemen to whom our hearts we devote
Is our dearest hope;

We erased the darkness with determined will
And with the National Unity we realised our dreams.

We marched towards the noble goal
With God's blessings and with steady steps.

Our people never yield to the tyranny of ages
And will stand firm to challenge the oppressors
And will live a dignified life.

YEMEN
People's Republic

No words

Music by
ABULQADER JAMAAKHAN (*b.* 1928)

Maestoso

First used on the occasion of the Independence of the People's Republic, 30 November, 1967.

YUGOSLAVIA

Words by
SAMUEL TOMAŠIK (1813-1887)

Composer unknown
Arr. by BORIVOJE SIMIĆ

Originally composed about the middle of the 19th. century as an anthem of the Slavonic movement for the Union of Slavs and after-wards adopted by some of the Slavonic countries as their National Anthem. It became the National Anthem of Yugoslavia in 1945.

Poland also has this tune for her National Anthem.

Ži - ve-će   ve - kov' - ma,   Za - lud pre - ti___ po -nor pa - kla,___

1. Za - lud va - tra   gro - ma,

2. Za - lud va - tra   gro - ma!

2. *Nek se sada i nad nama*
Burom sve raznese,
Stena puca, dub se lama,
Zemlja nek se trese.
Mi stojimo postojano
Kano klisurine;
Proklet bio izdajica⎱ *Repeat*
Svoje domovine! ⎰

Translation by Tomislav Tadin

1. Hey Slavs! our grandfathers' word still lives,
   As long as their sons' heart beats for the people.
   It lives, the spirit of Slavs lives, it will live for centuries,
   The abyss of hell threatens in vain, the fire of thunder is in vain.

2. Now let everything above us be carried away by the bura.*
   The rock cracks, the oak breaks, let the ground shake.
   We stand steadfastly like cliffs;
   Let the traitor of his homeland be damned!

*A fast and sudden north-east wind, which blows along the eastern Adriatic coast.

ZAÏRE

Words by
SIMON-PIERRE BOKA (*b.* 1929)

Music by
JOSEPH LUTUMBA
Arr. by T.M. CARTLEDGE

Broadly and firmly

Za - ï - rois, dans la paix_ re - trou - vée, Peuple u -

-ni, nous som - mes Za - ï - rois. En a - vant, fier et plein de di - gni-

Adopted in 1971.

al Qui nous re-lie aux a-ïeux, à nos en-fants: PAIX, JUS

-TICE et TRA-VAIL, PAIX, JUS-TICE et TRA-VAIL.

Translation

Zaïrians, in refound peace
We are a united people, Zaïrians.
Forward with pride and dignity,
A great people, for ever free!
O Tricolour, kindle the sacred fire in us
So that we may build our country finer yet,
Beside a "Kingly River",
Beside a "Kingly River".
Waving Tricolour, revive the ideal
Which binds us to our forbears and our children:
PEACE, JUSTICE and WORK,
PEACE, JUSTICE and WORK.

ZAMBIA

Words written collectively

Music by
MANKAYI ENOCH SONTONGA* (*d.* 1904)†
Arr. by Mrs. WALTERS and D.W. DUNN

With dignity

1. Stand and sing of Zam-bia, proud and free, Land of work and joy in
2. A - fri - ca is our own mo-ther-land, Fash-ion'd with and blessed by
3. One land and one na - tion is our cry, Dig - ni - ty and peace 'neath

u - ni - ty, Vic-tors in the strug - gle for the right,
God's good hand, Let us all her peo - ple join as one,
Zam - bia's sky, Like our no-ble ea - gle in its flight,

(S.T.) We've won

We have won freedom's fight. All one, strong and free.
Bro - thers un-der the sun. All one, strong and free.
Zam - bia, praise to thee. All one, strong and free.

(T.B.) in the sun.

CHORUS — Sung after 3rd Verse only

(S.) Praise be to God.
(A.T.) God.
(B.) Praise be, praise be, praise be,

Bless our great na -
na -
Zam - bia,

The music for this National Anthem was originally written as a hymn tune at Lovedale Mission in Cape Province, South Africa.

The tune became well known throughout a large part of southern, central and eastern Africa, and the words were translated into many African languages. Indeed, it came to be popularly known as the Bantu National Anthem. The tune was officially adopted by Tanganyika as its National Anthem on the achievement of independence in 1961. See also Zimbabwe. New words have been specially written for Zambia. A competition was held and these words were produced as a composite version after a study of the ideas and the words of the six leading entries in the competition.

† Year of birth unknown.

- -tion, Free men we stand____ Un -der the flag____
- -tion, Free men we stand____ Un -der the flag____
Zam - bia, Zam - bia, Free men we stand____ Un -der the flag____

of____ our land.____ Zam - bia, praise to____ thee!____

All   one,   strong____ and   free.____

1. *Lumbanyeni Zambia, no kwanga,*
   Ne cilumba twange tuumfwane,
   Mpalume sha bulwi bwa cine,
   Twaliilubula.
   Twikatane bonse.

2. *Bonse tuli bana ba Africa,*
   Uwasenaminwa na Lesa,
   Nomba bonse twendele pamo,
   Twaliilubula.
   Twikatane bonse.

3. *Fwe lukuta lwa Zambia lonse,*
   Twikatane tubyo mutende,
   Pamo nga lubambe mu mulu,
   Lumbanyeni Zambia.
   Twikatane bonse.

CHORUS (after 3rd verse only)
   Lumbanyeni,
   Lesa, Lesa, wesu,
   Apale calo,
   Zambia, Zambia, Zambia.
   Fwe bantungwa
   Mu luunga lwa calo.
      Lumbanyeni Zambia.
      Twikatane bonse.

ZIMBABWE

Music by
MANKAYI ENOCH SONTONGA* (*d.* 1904)†

ords written
ollectively

Moderato con dignità

f I - she - ko - mbo-re - ra A - fri - ca Nga - i - si - mu-dzi - rwe

zi - ta ra - yo____ I - nzwa-i mi - te - u - ro ye - du

I - she ko-mbo - re - ra,____ I - su, mhu-ri ya - yo.

Hu - ya mwe-ya____ Hu - ya mwe-ya____
Hu - ya mwe-ya ko-mbo-re-ra Hu - ya mwe-ya ko-mbo-re-ra
mp

he music is also used for the National Anthem of Tanzania and Zambia.
ee footnote to ZAMBIA for further details.
ear of birth unknown.

Hu - ya mwe -ya   Hu - ya mwe - ya   wo - u -tsve - ne

U - ti   ko -mbo- re - re   I - su   mhu- ri ya - yo.

Free Translation

God bless Africa,
Let her fame spread far and wide!
Hear our prayer:
May God bless us!

Come, Spirit, come!
Come! Holy Spirit!
Come and bless us, her children!

NATIONAL DAYS

AFGHANISTAN	27 May	Independence Day, 1919
ALBANIA	11 January	National Day, 1946
ALGERIA	5 July	Independence Day, 1962
	1 November	National Day, 1954
ANDORRA	8 September	Jungfrau von Meritxell Day (Patron Saint of Andorra), 1874
ANGOLA	11 November	Independence Day, 1975
ANTIGUA and BARBUDA	1 November	Independence Day, 1981
ARGENTINA	25 May	National Day, 1810
	9 July	Independence Day, 1816
AUSTRALIA	26 January	Australia Day, 1788
	25 April	Anzac Day, 1915
AUSTRIA	15 May	Signing of Austrian State Treaty, 1955
	26 October	National Day, 1955
BAHAMAS	10 July	Independence Day, 1973
BAHRAIN	15 August	Independence Day, 1971
BANGLADESH	16 December	Constitution Day, 1972
BARBADOS	30 November	Independence Day, 1966
BELGIUM	21 July	Independence Day, 1831
	7 September	Birthday of H.M. King Baudouin, 1930
BELIZE	21 September	Independence Day, 1981
BENIN	30 November	Independence Day, 1975
BHUTAN	11 November	Birthday of H.M. King Jigme Singye Wangchuck, 1955
BOLIVIA	9 April	Anniversary of the National Revolution, 1952
	6 August	Anniversary of Independence, 1825
BOTSWANA	30 September	Independence Day, 1966
BOURKINA FASO	5 August	Independence Day, 1960
	11 December	National Day, 1958
BRAZIL	7 September	Independence Day, 1822
BRUNEI	1 January	Independence Day, 1984
BULGARIA	9 September	National Day, 1944
BURMA	4 January	Independence Day, 1948
	12 February	Union Day, 1947
BURUNDI	1 July	Independence Day, 1962
CAMEROON	1 January	Independence Day, 1960
CANADA	1 July	Canada Day, 1867
CAPE VERDE ISLANDS	5 July	Independence Day, 1975
CENTRAL AFRICAN REPUBLIC	13 August	Independence Day, 1960
CHAD	11 August	Independence Day, 1960
CHILE	18 September	Independence Day, 1810
CHINA	1 October	Proclamation of Provisional Constitution, 1949
COLOMBIA	20 July	Independence Day, 1810
COMORO ISLANDS	6 July	Independence Day, 1975
CONGO	15 August	Independence Day, 1960
COSTA RICA	15 September	Independence Day, 1821
CUBA	1 January	National Day, 1959
CYPRUS	16 August	Independence Day, 1960
CZECHOSLOVAKIA	28 October	Foundation of Czechoslovak Republic, 1918
DENMARK	16 April	Birthday of H.M. Queen Margrethe II, 1940
	5 June	Constitution Day, 1849
DJIBOUTI	27 June	Independence Day, 1977
DOMINICA	3 November	Independence Day, 1978
DOMINICAN REPUBLIC	27 February	Independence Day, 1844
ECUADOR	10 August	Independence Day, 1809
EGYPT	23 July	National Day, 1952
EL SALVADOR	15 September	Independence Day, 1821
ENGLAND	23 April	St. George's Day
EQUATORIAL GUINEA	12 October	Independence Day, 1968
ETHIOPIA	12 September	National Day, 1974

FIJI	10 October	Independence Day, 1970
FINLAND	6 December	Independence Day, 1917
FRANCE	14 July	National Day (Bastille Day, 1789)
GABON	17 August	Independence Day, 1960
GAMBIA, THE	18 February	Independence Day, 1965
GERMANY (East)	7 October	Constitution Day, 1949
GERMANY (West)	17 June	Day of Unity, 1954
GHANA	6 March	Independence Day, 1957
GREAT BRITAIN	21 April	Birthday of H.M. Queen Elizabeth II, 1926
GREECE	25 March	Independence Day, 1821
GRENADA	7 February	Independence Day, 1974
GUATEMALA	15 September	Independence Day, 1821
GUINEA	2 October	Proclamation of the Republic, 1958
GUINEA – BISSAU	10 September	Independence Day, 1974
GUYANA	26 May	Independence Day, 1966
HAITI	1 January	Independence Day, 1804
HONDURAS	15 September	Independence Day, 1821
HUNGARY	4 April	Anniversary of the Liberation, 1945
ICELAND	17 June	Anniversary of Establishment of the Republic, 1944
	1 December	Independence Day, 1918
INDIA	26 January	Republic Day, 1950
	15 August	Independence Day, 1947
INDONESIA	17 August	Independence Day, 1945
IRAN	1 April	Islamic Republic Day, 1979
IRAQ	14 July	National Day, 1958
IRISH REPUBLIC	17 March	St. Patrick's Day
ISLE OF MAN	5 July	National Day, 1752
ISRAEL	15 May	Independence Day, 1948
ITALY	2 June	Anniversary of Proclamation of the Republic, 1946
IVORY COAST	7 December	Independence Day, 1960
JAMAICA	6 August	Independence Day, 1962 *(This is celebrated the First Monday of August each year)*
JAPAN	29 April	Birthday of H.M. Emperor Hirohito, 1901
	3 May	Constitution Day, 1947
JORDAN	25 May	Independence Day, 1946
	14 November	Birthday of H.M. King Hussein, 1935
KAMPUCHEA	17 April	National Day, 1976
KENYA	12 December	Independence Day, 1963 and Republic Day, 1964
KIRIBATI	12 July	Independence Day, 1979
KOREA (North)	9 September	Constitution Day, 1948
KOREA (South)	15 August	Independence Day, 1948
KUWAIT	19 June	National Day, 1961
LAOS	11 May	National Day (Constitution Day), 1947
	19 July	Independence Day, 1946
LEBANON	22 November	Independence Day, 1943
LESOTHO	4 October	Independence Day, 1966
LIBERIA	26 July	Independence Day, 1847
LIBYAN ARAB JAMAHIRIYA	1 September	National Day, 1969
LIECHTENSTEIN	16 August	Birthday of H.S.H. Prince Franz-Josef II, 1906
LUXEMBOURG	23 June	National Day, 1962
MALAGASY	26 June	Proclamation of Independence of the Republic, 1960
MALAWI	6 July	Independence Day, 1964 and Republic Day, 1966
MALAYSIA	31 August	National Day, 1957
MALDIVES	26 July	Independence Day, 1965

MALI	22 September	Independence Day, 1960
MALTA	31 March	Freedom Day, 1979
MAURITANIA	28 November	Independence Day, 1960
MAURITIUS	12 March	Independence Day, 1968
MEXICO	16 September	National Day, 1810
MONACO	31 May	Birthday of H.S.H. Prince Rainier III, 1923
	19 November	National Day (St. Rainier Day), 1949
MONGOLIA	11 July	National Day, 1921
MOROCCO	9 July	Birthday of H.M. King Hassan II, 1929
	18 November	Independence Day, 1956
MOZAMBIQUE	25 June	Independence Day, 1975
NAURU	1 February	Independence Day, 1968
NEPAL	18 February	National Day, 1952
	28 December	Birthday of H.M. King Birendra, 1945
NETHERLANDS	31 January	Birthday of H.M. Queen Beatrix, 1938
NEW ZEALAND	6 February	New Zealand Day, 1840
	25 April	Anzac Day, 1915
NICARAGUA	15 September	Independence Day, 1821
NIGER	3 August	Independence Day, 1960
	18 December	National Day, 1958
NIGERIA	1 October	Independence Day, 1960
NORWAY	17 May	Constitution Day, 1814
	2 July	Birthday of H.M. King Olav V, 1903
OMAN	18 July	Oman Day, 1971. First anniversary of the accession of H.M. Sultan Qaboos
PAKISTAN	23 March	Republic Day, 1956
	14 August	Independence Day, 1947
PANAMA	3 November	Independence Day, 1903
PAPUA NEW GUINEA	16 September	Independence Day, 1975
PARAGUAY	14 May	Independence Day, 1811
	25 November	Constitution Day, 1870
PERU	28 July	Independence Day, 1821
PHILIPPINES	4 July	Independence Day, 1946
POLAND	22 July	Constitution Day, 1952
PORTUGAL	10 June	National Day, 1880
QATAR	1 September	Independence Day, 1971
ROMANIA	9 May	National Independence Day, 1877
	23 August	Anniversary of the Liberation, 1944
RWANDA	1 July	Independence Day, 1962
SAINT KITTS and NEVIS	19 September	Independence Day, 1983
SAINT LUCIA	22 February	Independence Day, 1979
SAINT VINCENT	27 October	Independence Day, 1979
SAN MARINO	3 September	National Day
SÃO TOMÉ and PRÍNCIPE	12 July	Independence Day, 1975
SAUDI ARABIA	20 May	Independence Day, 1927
	23 September	National Day, 1964
SCOTLAND	30 November	St. Andrew's Day
SENEGAL	4 April	Independence Day, 1960
SEYCHELLES	29 June	Independence Day, 1976
SIERRA LEONE	19 April	Constitution Day, 1971
SINGAPORE	9 August	Independence Day, 1965
SOLOMON ISLANDS	7 July	Independence Day, 1978
SOMALIA	1 July	Independence Day, 1960
SOUTH AFRICA	31 May	Republic Day, 1961
SPAIN	5 January	Birthday of H.M. King Juan Carlos, 1938
SRI LANKA	4 February	Independence Day, 1948
SUDAN	1 January	Independence Day, 1956
SURINAM	25 November	Independence Day, 1975
SWAZILAND	6 September	Independence Day, 1968

SWEDEN	30 April	Birthday of H.M. King Carl XVI Gustaf, 1946
	6 June	National Day, 1809
SWITZERLAND	1 August	Anniversary of the Foundation of Confederation, 1291
SYRIA	17 April	National Day, 1943
TAIWAN	10 October	Proclamation of Republic of Dr. Sun Yat-Sen, 1911
TANZANIA	26 April	Tanzanian Union Day, 1964
	9 December	Independence Day, 1961 and Republic Day, 1962
THAILAND	5 December	Birthday of H.M. King Bhumibol Adulyadej, 1927
TOGO	27 April	Independence Day, 1960
TONGA	4 June	Independence Day, 1970
	4 July	Birthday of H.M. King Tupou IV, 1918
TRINIDAD and TOBAGO	31 August	National Day, 1962
TUNISIA	1 June	National Day, 1959
	25 July	Anniversary of Proclamation of the Republic, 1957
TURKEY	29 October	Proclamation of the Republic, 1923
TUVALU	1 October	Independence Day, 1978
UGANDA	9 October	Independence Day, 1962
UNION OF SOVIET SOCIALIST REPUBLICS	7 November	Anniversary of the October Socialist Revolution, 1917
UNITED ARAB EMIRATES	2 December	Independence Day, 1971
UNITED STATES OF AMERICA	4 July	Independence Day, 1776
	27 November	Thanksgiving Day, 1621 *(This is celebrated the Fourth Thursday of November each year)*
URUGUAY	25 August	Independence Day, 1825
VANUATU	30 July	Independence Day, 1980
VATICAN CITY STATE	18 May	Birthday of H.H. Pope John Paul II, 1920
VENEZUELA	5 July	National Day (Signing of Independence, 1811)
VIETNAM	2 September	National Day, 1945
WALES	1 March	St. David's Day
WESTERN SAMOA	1 January	Independence Day, 1962
YEMEN (Arab Republic)	26 September	National Day, 1962
YEMEN (People's Republic)	30 November	Independence Day, 1967
YUGOSLAVIA	29 November	National Day, 1945
ZAÏRE	30 June	Independence Day, 1960
ZAMBIA	24 October	Independence Day, 1964
ZIMBABWE	18 April	Independence Day, 1980